The Baroness, the Scribe,
and the Camel-Driver

Written and Illustrated by
Jane B. Brundage

The Baroness, the Scribe, and the Camel-Driver.
Written and illustrated by Jane B. Brundage.

Copyright (C) 1995
by Jane B. Brundage.

The author of this book is not medically trained, and cannot assume responsibility for the use and application of any technique or information, medical or psychological, mentioned herein. The intent of this book is to describe the impact which certain alternative methods of healing had on the author herself, and should not, therefore, be construed as medical advice. It is suggested that the reader seek the professional expertise of a physician or psychotherapist for an opinion on which methods of healing are appropriate for him.

Cover design by Jane B. Brundage
Author's photograph by Tad Brundage

Library of Congress Catalog Card Number 95-92624
ISBN 0-9649017-0-6

Printed by Mystic Publications, Mystic, CT.

ACKNOWLEDGEMENTS

I would like to thank all the individuals who have given their support to the writing of this book, whether directly or indirectly. In particular, I am grateful to Marion Davis, for her guidance through the regressions contained in the book; my husband, Tad, for his faith in me, and for his help in getting the book published; my children, Ryan and Seth, for graciously allowing me time away from them in which to write and create; my brother, Bracken, for his careful editing of the manuscript; and, my friend and colleague, Nancy Grasso, for her generous help with the additional regression work I needed to complete the book. My love and thanks to you all.

To loved ones,
past and present,
many of whom walk the pages of this book,
those dear, sweet souls,
who have lovingly lent part of the living of their own lives,
to my living of mine.

Introduction

When I speak of past lives, a lot of people are surprised to find out that normally we have quite a number of them. Though I have no idea how many lifetimes I have actually spent on earth, I did have the occasion, about five years ago, to acquaint myself with about twenty previous incarnations, an experience which I gained through what is known as past-life regression therapy (hereafter sometimes referred to as PLT). In the beginning of 1990, I began regression therapy with the help of a past-life practitioner named Marion Davis. My motive in doing so stemmed from what I felt were unsatisfactory experiences with more traditional methods of psychotherapy and periods of professional counseling which had failed to bring any sort of lasting relief from oftentimes unmanageable periods of depression, mood swings, and emotional turmoil.

By the end of a six-month period in regression therapy, however, I experienced a lot of clearing away of some long-standing emotional issues, and was feeling very pleased with the progress I had made. When I discovered quite accidentally that I was capable of obtaining past-life information through meditation, without the assistance of a guide, I decided to complete my formal therapy. In leaving it, though, I felt that so much had been given to me because of my experiences with PLT, that I began to write a book about it.

This book has been through its own series of transformations, and it has grown as I have over the last five years. I started to write it because I felt I had gained something more than just a new inner calm from the past-life regressions. The therapy was so powerful, I found myself experiencing some substantial spill-over into certain metaphysical and spiritual considerations. It made me start to wonder about the big picture, to ask the kinds of questions people seem to be asking themselves more and more these days, questions like: Who am I? What am I doing here? Who created me? *Is* there a God? What is the meaning of my life? How can I take optimum advantage of the opportunity I have right now in this life I'm living?

The spiritual quest that spiraled out of my therapy five years ago has also needed to find its place in this book, so as I have learned new things, I have returned to the text time and again to include them. I've found that as time has gone on, the book has continued to come closer to what I had really wanted to say all along. I have learned much in the writing of it, and it is my hope that perhaps some individual who reads the book, even if he doesn't readily embrace the notion of reincarnation, will come away with some insights of his own.

What Is Past-Life Regression?

Whenever people hear of my work on this book, they often ask me what I really think about reincarnation, and whether I believe that the lives I uncovered during the regression process were real. There are several possible explanations I could give for what is being experienced by a person who is *regressed*.

First, we could say that, perhaps the soul reincarnates into a series of lifetimes for the purpose of realizing its own progression or growth through experience, and that any or all of these lifetimes can be recalled during hypnosis or some other trance state by the soul that has experienced them.

Secondly, we might say that more important and obvious than the progression of the *individual*, there is progression of the human race, and are we not in some ways, manifestations of our own collective growth, or what Jungians refer to as the *collective consciousness*? Following this line of thinking, we might say then, that what we recall is not necessarily personal experience but *an* experience, an event, a life which is tapped from the collective human memory because it is appropriate to the situation at hand.

A third possibility is that the regression material is *unconsciously* created, a quasi-dream or self-composed episode, which evokes the core emotional content of an individual's harbored and suppressed pain, drawing it out through pure suggestive imagery, just as a nightmare can make one bolt awake to find his heart racing and his body in a sweat.

I see validity in each viewpoint, and I feel reluctant to rule out any one of them as a possible answer to the question of what really does happen when someone is regressed. Over time, I have come to believe that the answer lies somewhere within all three possibilities, i.e, that we progress spiritually both individually and collectively through time, and that the information from that experience is at all times available to each of us. I believe that some part of us belongs to ourselves as a unique and special creation of a Supreme Being, while some part of us belongs to the universal or God consciousness, and that this heritage makes us by nature all-knowing, all-powerful and all-good.

I believe that being made in God's image means that we have a power or essence which cannot be diminished or compromised by any experience, including death, and that we have the free will to continually create new existences for ourselves. In a sense, we are at all moments completely self-contained and self-sufficient, and do not ever have the need—though we believe we do—to seek answers or insight into our problems *outside* of ourselves. I think that within we carry all of the wisdom and power necessary to teach and heal ourselves, and that we innately *know* how to alter our present state of existence on any level. That is why it is not phenomenal, but completely natural, that information about our past lives and the wisdom gained from past-life experiences are so accessible, as ordinary and close at hand as a dream or a childhood memory.

But, for the purposes of this book, the emphasis will be somewhat single-minded, presenting the regression process as simply an unfolding of *past lives*, or, if you will, historical events in the progressive life of the reincarnated soul. This is what I believed I was experiencing at the time of my regression therapy, and since that is the premise under which the sessions later became intellectually, emotionally, and spiritually comprehensible to me, that is the premise under which they are explained here.

What I don't believe, however, is that the experiences rendered through past-life regression are in any way *conscious* creation. For one who has experienced the process, it is very clear that the conscious mind is incapable of creating or even, in many cases, second-guessing the meaning behind the images which appear in the mind during regression.

Furthermore, the emotional impact of the recall, as well as the therapeutic value drawn out of the PLT experience are very real, very tangible, and lasting. In essence, it doesn't really matter whether such and such a person really lived at such and such a time if the experience of *being* that individual—if even for a moment—brings with it the realized benefit of relief—relief from anger and guilt and unhappiness, from pain both emotional and physical—as well as insight into problems that are life-long, and a long-awaited feeling of lightness and well-being.

The realized benefits of past-life regression therapy are not unique to me. This therapy is fast becoming recognized in the psychiatric community as a very powerful and effective tool. Results are typically immediate, dynamic and enduring, and though few people stay with an extensive course of past-life therapy, as I did, many have felt remarkable impact from just one or two regression sessions.

The World According to Jane

My experiences with past-life regression therapy changed the way I used to think about a lot of things, and I know my beliefs are unusual. I did not write this book with the intention of converting anyone to my way of thinking, or *proving* that I have lived before. I have simply tried here to record and explain all of what I learned through my past-life experiences about myself, the people I love, and the world we share with everyone else.

People have their own versions of how the world works and what we're all doing here on this planet. More precisely, we all *need* our own version, and my suggestion to anyone who reads this book is *continue to hang on to whatever explanation feels right.*

I know it is a stretch for some people to consider the possibility that they have lived before. Or, even more staggering, the probability that they will live again. Even though we believe that the bodies we live in right now will someday cease to operate, it's odd to imagine that we—the individual spirit energies within these bodies—will go on. It is hard to envision ourselves separating from the concrete space we call the self, and inhabiting the space of an entirely different body at an entirely different time.

For instance, if I were to try and describe how I see myself in the world today, I would probably say something like, well, there is this individual, female, 42 years old, living in Connecticut, married with two children. She has dark hair and blue eyes, and she is writing a book, a book about other people she has been. In this life, she is called Jane.

Within the physical space known to herself and others as Jane, there is a spirit, or what some refer to as the soul, what others might call the Higher self. This Higher self is ageless, holding within it the knowledge and experience of centuries. This Higher self understands its purpose in becoming the personality Jane for this limited and finite experience called her life. The spirit within Jane is both constant and transmutable, and it will alter itself, as required, once the life that is Jane's reaches completion.

However, in all likelihood, when this spirit returns to earth the next time, as some new personality, there will be some repetition of the challenges, problems and emotional experiences that were Jane's. The focus of this spirit's next life will most likely be the issues which failed to reach resolution during the lifetime experienced as Jane. The physical components of this new life will also change, i.e., sex, race, nationality, personality, physical appearance, religion, culture, economic circumstances, and so on. But all of these changes will be made for the expressed purpose of learning and experiencing more fully what has already been experienced so far.

The other actors in Jane's life—her husband, parents, siblings, friends, and children—may also reappear in this new life. They will shift roles, in all likelihood, like members of an acting troupe, who perfect their craft by assuming new characters and circumstances with each different play they perform. Parent may become child; husband, wife; sibling, parent, and so on. And then again, the spirit who currently experiences life on earth as Jane, might not return at all.

Coming to earth and existing for a time on this plane under a particular set of circumstances, a process which we call *life*, is only one of the things we are capable of doing as spirit forms. Being in pure spirit state, the condition which occurs before, after and between lives on earth, is our true and natural state.* Living on the earth is for us as spirits secondary, temporary, completely elective, experimental, and *experiential.* By that, I mean quite simply that coming to earth is an opportunity which we are given as spiritual entities in order to *experience* the emotional and physical planes which make up the human condition. It is not a required experience by any means, but I suppose like the climbing of Mount Everest, we do it because it's there.

One of the biggest problems people seem to have with the notion of reincarnation is that it seems so fruitless and repetitious, that we live lifetime after lifetime rehashing the same issues, and that after centuries of pain and anguish, it never seems to get us anywhere.

To me it's helpful to keep in mind that our overriding aim in coming here is to *experience*—good or bad, fruitful or not. As humans, operating out of conscious mind, we tend to evaluate behavior, objects, people and events, because it orders our existence.

But within the God consciousness—or the mind of the Creator—things do not differ in value. To assign value to something requires judgment, and our Creator is not a judge, but both an observer of, and a participant in, all human experience. So, to really grasp the meaning of our numerous and varied existences on earth, we have to suspend our urge to evaluate life and its experiences as good, bad or indifferent. They just *are.*

---

*I do not wish to imply, however, that being in the body is in any way an inferior or imperfect state of being. All experiences rendered to us as spirit forms have impact and importance, and all of our choices—even though we often find it hard to see them that way—are perfect ones.

Secondly, we *do* progress. One only needs to look at the history of the human race (which in universe years is a mere wink of time), its evolution and growing intricacy to realize that. In some ways, it may seem we are repeating experience, but each time a lesson is repeated, it is realized on a deeper and more complex level, just as, for instance, the history of the Civil War might be taught more than once throughout a child's education, each time becoming more detailed and challenging in content.

We also need to keep in mind that getting ourselves locked in repetitive drama of some form or other, whether it spans a lifetime or centuries of lifetimes is not a given, but an option. There is, after all, security and safety in repetition. Why change plays and be faced with learning a whole new set of lines, exits and entrances, when you can just stay with the one you've been starring in for the last 1200 years?

Lastly, I think it's important to emphasize that we do come here by choice. Each individual's Higher self is the chief architect of his life experience, and though the reigning personality may be completely out of touch with the grand design of its current existence, it might help to remember, that at heart, each of us is steadfastly devoted to carrying out each mission we are given on this earth. As we are to the people and experiences we have known while being here. And *that* is why we continue to come back.

I have heard it said a few times by some people who embrace the idea of reincarnation that they intend to get it right this time so that they won't *have* to come back. With all due respect, I believe they are missing the point entirely. *We really are here because we want to be*, and our Earth experience is by no means mandatory. The soul directs its own experience here, and actually delights in the miraculous process of its learning and evolution. Life on the planet Earth, in the eyes of the soul, is never viewed as a drudgery, or something to be gotten beyond. And any soul who might conceivably be evolved enough to be nearing resolution of its Earth experience would, by contrast, be so at peace with the wisdom of its process, it would have no impulse whatsoever to question how much longer the experience was going to last, or desire that it to be completed. It would, in fact, be somewhat unrealistic to assume that given the choice—as indeed we will be—we would ever opt to bow out now, just when we're finally rounding the bend.

A New Terminology

In writing this book I use a lot of terms that most people will find new and confusing. So for the ease of discussion I'm going to spend some time here elaborating on my understanding and use of these terms. Some of the words and concepts I mention in the book are ones you might hear in ordinary conversation, but I find that certain words carry different meanings for different people, and so for the sake of clarity it's better if I make it understood what meaning they carry in *my* mind.

Within the text of this book I will use the term *ego* interchangeably with the word *personality* to describe an individual's current incarnation, i.e., the conscious self as one is aware of it. It is a combination of how a person defines who she is in the world, the description she would give to her character, and the person she sees when she looks in the mirror.

That self is, as I see it, a manifestation of what is often called the *Higher self.* (I often use this term in conjunction with the word *soul*, though I realize they are not the same thing. Technically, the soul is simply a record of the Higher self's Earth-related experience. For purposes of discussion about past-lives, however, I find they sometimes go hand in hand.)

I have also seen what I call Higher self referred to by others as the God-self, the in-dwelling God, the spirit within, and the creative consciousness, but whatever you personally term it, the way I define it is this: Higher self is a unique and singular expression of God. It is one facet or example (within an infinite number of capabilities and possibilities) of our Creator's consciousness *manifesting out* in order to know and experience Itself. It follows without question that the beneficence, power and omniscience of the Creator's consciousness are also particular to all that is manifested out of it, and so, consequently, the Higher self is nothing less than Divinity, miraculously and permanently resident in all of us.

Higher self is true self. The rest of the package—the body, the personality, the prior incarnations—is just there to enable the creative expression of the Higher self in its desire to evolve the soul, just as the cocoon exists to enable the butterfly.

Obviously, experience is perceived quite differently by the Higher self and the personality: the personality, which is limited in its thinking, is judgmental of its experience, burdened by regret from the past and fear of the future; the Higher self, which is infinitely knowing, is judgmental of nothing and unencumbered by time.

To the personality, experience is *dualistic*, that is, both negative and positive, blissful and terrible, turbulent and calm. It is caught in the sway of these opposites, forever trying to determine on which side of the seesaw everything is falling. The personality rails against the duality and calls its world an imperfect one.

The Higher self, however, sees that the duality is there only for the purpose of evolution. It is a game and challenge by which the Higher self is never daunted, but is only kept curious and fascinated. The Higher self accepts the duality for what it is—the possibility for polarized experiences to exist simultaneously—and thinks no more of it. Dualism, in other words, is not an either-or experience; it is living both negative and positive at the same time, because they cannot be separated out from one another. Being in duality means we sit not at either end of the seesaw, but at the center.

Now, in any discussion of reincarnation, you will hear the word *karma* bandied about. My view of karma is that it is nothing more than ongoing challenge, something that is not yet fully learned or understood. Karma represents the evolution of a thought through dualistic experience. If a learning has not been completed in one lifetime, it will appear in subsequent lives, repeatedly, under different guises perhaps, until it is recognized, understood and released. When someone says this challenge is karmic, it means, I've done this before; there's a long history attached to this.

Karma is neither good nor bad; it simply flavors and enhances the dualistic experience. It is the history that gives present-day reality its shape and dimension. It gives the seesaw of life its momentum.

Though I have heard some people suggest it, we are not actually *victims* of our karma. Granted, it is not something that can be avoided in life, but it is there to fuel the soul's evolution. Our repeated efforts to avoid karma is what ends up prolonging it for us.

Dissolution of karma is more readily achieved by accepting and embracing our emotional challenges, rather than denying them. By that, I mean acceptance to the point where there is no longer any blame or fear or doubt or emotional equivocation of any kind surrounding the issue itself. It is acceptance to the point where one no longer holds any thought about a given experience, which is in any way dualistic. When one can pull himself out of dualistic thinking and judgment, he has entered a reality where karma does not exist.

Why Past-Life Regression Works

What are the karmic issues in your own life, you might wonder? How do you confront these issues if you don't even know what they are?

There are those who will argue that *everything* in life is karmic, and I agree that this is on some level true, but for the sake of discussion here, let's just say that quite typically, a karmic issue is one which is the sorest and most difficult for you. It is an issue that tends to web out into every aspect of your life. It comes up in your relationships, in your career, even in your health.

For example, suppose one of your karmic challenges surrounds the issue of self-confidence. You may hold the belief that others are smarter or more creative than you; you may have performance anxieties, fears of failure, or perfectionistic tendencies. Perhaps you give up too easily and abandon the projects you start. You are quick to say: Oh, I could never do something like that. I don't know enough. Or, I'm not strong enough to handle that.

There is thought and emotion that underpins this pattern of behavior. It is perhaps the belief that you don't deserve to succeed or that something bad will happen to you if you do. With these thoughts are attached certain emotions, such as self-hatred or fear. These thoughts and emotions keep the pattern a-spin. You try, you sabotage yourself, you fail, you reaffirm your belief about yourself.

Recently, it has become the theory of a growing number of therapists and mental health practitioners that the secret to breaking up these patterns of behavior lies rooted in past-life experience, even though memory of prior existences is typically not conscious.

But, at any moment in time, our *unconscious* mind is voicing a thousand different messages to us about a thousand different subjects, and within this process, past-life experience is supremely powerful in dictating how we feel today, how we view the world now, why we choose to spend our time with certain people, and why we make the career and life decisions we do. Why? Because that *is* our experience, what we have learned and what we know about life on this planet.

Therefore, trying to solve karmic issues with just the tool of conscious memory is like trying to assess the stature of a business by looking at only the last fiscal year of its performance. It may be the most relevant and timely data available, but it is by no means the whole story. And it will not tell you how the business got to where it is now.

I like to use the metaphor *emotional baggage*, because I think it describes karmic experience in a really succinct way. Karma *is* baggage, and what past-life regression therapy gives us is the key to the steamer trunk. It lets us open up the lid and see just what it is that's making the blasted thing so heavy in the first place. It allows us to unearth the contents bit by bit, identify to whom each scrap of memory, every shred of resentment, each speck of hatred, and mantle of fear belongs. And then, best of all, it gives us the opportunity to off-load it all. "This isn't important anymore," we have the chance to now assert, "and it should no longer have any power over me."

If someone were to ask me to describe precisely how this therapy made me feel, I'd say: "five hundred pounds lighter." I'm not trying to be

facetious in my use of that particular terminology. Emotionally speaking,
I mean it quite literally.

How Past Life Regression Works

A common concern which many people have about the regression process
is: shouldn't this information be left alone?   If we don't remember,
perhaps we weren't meant to tamper with it?
   At the risk of seeming too obvious, we actually *do* remember our past
lives. What is probably a more accurate term is that this information is,
of necessity, *repressed*. I say of necessity, because to hold full conscious
memory of all the details of our past lives would be a debilitating, chaotic,
and actually quite pointless way for us to live.
   Sometimes, however, like all things repressed from the conscious mind,
past-life trauma becomes potent and suggestive enough to hamper your
current life and behavior. In the areas where that infiltration occurs, and
becomes problematic, PLT can be a useful and expedient tool in defusing
it.
   But over and above all that, I think it's important to emphasize that we
do *own* this information. It belongs to us as much as any event or detail
of our present existence, and to divorce it from ourselves emotionally and
psychologically, as if it were something either forbidden or undesirable, is
to seriously underestimate ourselves and the collective experience that has
made us who we are.
   If distress from past-life trauma is making itself felt in the present, then
somewhere there is a deep-seated desire to have it investigated, and I
would suggest that a generally wise way to live is to never discount what
the inner self finds important. Repressed emotion and experience are like
petulant little children: the more you ignore them, the more obnoxious
they will get.
   Frankly, we should feel no more emotional repugnance toward our past
lives, than we should feel towards the image that looks back at us from the
mirror everyday or the dreams we have while asleep every night. They
are an essential and unremovable piece of what we are.
   Another very real concern that people sometimes have going into the
process is whether they will uncover something they either don't want to
know or won't be able to handle. It's a legitimate concern, but an
unlikely turn of events. The reason for this is two-fold. First, the
conscious mind works as a built-in filter for volatile information that is
either being held within or channeled out of the unconscious. This is why
we hear of cases of abused children who sometimes actually don't
remember their childhood trauma until they reach mid-life.   The

psychological theory behind this time lapse is that this information has not been permitted to filter through because the individual has not previously felt it was safe to do so.

Secondly, we need to remember that the unconscious mind is very literal in its interpretation of the questions we pose to it. If we approach it with a motive to heal, it will provide what is needed to do that. Because we do not desire to be frightened and traumatized by revelations from the past, we will not be presented with information we cannot assimilate.

Many people resist the idea that past-life information is so accessible. I think they like to believe that it's so buried and entrenched that you need the help of a deep hypnotic trance, a shot of sodium pentothal and a couple of crowbars to get it out. Not so. As one becomes more comfortable with the process, and one believes more fully in the mind's ability to provide such information, access becomes incredibly easy. It is quite reasonable to expect past-life material to unfold out of a relaxed, meditative state.

It's normal, in the beginning, to discredit what you are seeing and what the unconscious is revealing to you. With time and practice, that changes, and the typical response is for people to be completely amazed by the depth of their emotional reactions to past-life material, even while they are simultaneously mistrusting the factuality of it. That deep and unexpected emotional response is, I think, what convinces them in the end, that they're *not* making it up.

All of the transcripts in this book were produced under a meditative state, and not with the aid of hypnosis. I was guided into these meditative states by my therapist, and during them, I was, at all times, fully conscious of who I was, where I was and what I was doing. Past-life details were nonetheless accessible, and the curative affects of the sessions lasting and real. You can say what you will about the process, about reincarnation and the probability of past lives or an after-life. Whatever the conclusions you draw, that this process can solve problems, dissolve confusion and pain, lighten the spirit and off-load the burdens commonly carried through life is an indisputable fact. How or why that happens is actually immaterial.

As I've said before, our past-life history is much more accessible than most of us would imagine. While it may be comforting for some of us to believe otherwise, past-life information and associations spill into our present lives everyday: through our reactions to people and situations, through the choices we make, through the emotional connections we have with others in our lives, and even through our dreams. The truth is, we can't escape who we really are.

For the novice to regression, the process seems intimidating, and even threatening. In my own case, I found that those feelings came solely from a lack of familiarity with the process itself. Over time, as my comfort level naturally increased, the sessions proved easier and the material rendered from them less confusing and disjointed.

While regression material is readily available to all, I would suggest that reliance on a trained past-life therapist or guide is crucial, especially for a beginner. A therapist will help decipher the images you are seeing and the feelings you are experiencing. She can also lend to the session the necessary reassurance and objective insight you will often require along the way.

Before I was regressed for the first time, I imagined that the process would be something like dreaming or watching a movie unfold. But past-life regression is visually not nearly so clear or precise as that. Generally, information or responses to questions tend to come in a series of brief mental flashes or images. Sometimes it is a picture; sometimes it is a thought, sometimes an emotion or a sensation.

Initially in the process, one is guided back to the distant past, to any place and time which might hold significance to the problem or issue he wishes to better understand. Next, he is asked to begin to get a sense of who he was then: by way of dress, sex, age, demeanor or status. As each flash comes, an understanding begins to build. One may, for instance, have the sense he is on a farm, through flashes of terrain, or animals, or a tool he can feel in his hand. Mentally, he might experience the sensation of a warm breeze on his face or smell freshly-tilled dirt.

The recalled lifetime and its significance to the problem at hand—as you will gather from reading the transcripts—are pieced together from a series of "significant parts," which the subject accesses and reveals to the therapist or guide. This is sort of like a scene change in a play. Images may lighten or grow darker as you move from inside a cabin to the outside, or vice versa. You may suddenly feel cold and start physically shaking because you have moved to a scene where you are standing knee-deep in snow.

As you proceed through the significant parts of a past life, the object is to gather enough information to connect these experiences with the problem you are trying to address. The measure to which you are successful with that depends on a lot of things, but most importantly, your own receptivity to the information.

It also depends on how comfortable and practiced you are with the process, how complex and multi-layered the problem is, and how much time you are willing to spend afterward working the information through in your mind to determine more fully and clearly its connection to the existing problem.

I found that the rewards I gained from past-life therapy were largely due to the fact that I stuck with it. Early on, I recognized that what was happening during the sessions was affecting me in very real ways, and though I wasn't initially able to articulate why or how that was, I was willing to keep working at it until I could. And it was from that commitment that I reaped the real rewards.

The Importance of Forgiveness

Once the past-life memory, and more importantly the emotions attached to it, are reclaimed, a process of release and clearance can begin. Usually, this is accomplished through formally forgiving the actions of the self and the actions of others (who in some way brought harm to you), a process which takes place at the close of each particular past-life recall. The act of forgiveness permits clearance from the soul memory of dualistically-charged emotions, which you failed to release before exiting your past life.

I suppose it would be natural to wonder why this forgiveness or reconciliation would not occur at the end of each life when the soul is returned to the spirit world. Well, actually there's no need. As I've suggested before, once we reach an out-of-body state, we no longer evaluate and view experience through the veil of our earthly social consciousness (duality), and therefore, we no longer judge as right or wrong any experience, whether it is rendered by our own actions or the actions of others. Through the loving, all-knowing eyes of our Higher self, we will view even the most treacherous of acts as no more or less than a thing which was thought and created and therefore, existed. There is no requirement to forgive at this juncture, because the Higher self is incapable of the judgment which is prerequisite to the act of forgiveness.

Once, however, the individual assumes a new ego, he will once again learn to view experience through the filter of social consciousness in which he is raised. And he will automatically evaluate—often quite harshly—all experience, past and present, personal and interpersonal, natural and unnatural, which comes his way. As he begins, for instance, to encounter rejection and failure, he may recall—albeit unconsciously—other lifetimes when these experiences occurred, and call up the same emotions of anger, low self-esteem and unforgivingness he once felt.

I would say that what PLT does—by putting these issues and their history out on the table—is provide the opportunity to disconnect some of these entrenched emotions, which are leading one into continued intolerance of himself and others. The act of finishing, or releasing the karmic energy retained by the individual, is accomplished not so much by the mere surfacing of old issues, but directly and specifically through the process of forgiveness.

Forgiving ourselves and others for the losses, pain and entanglements of the past is the single most important act we perform in this or any life. We often find it difficult to accomplish, most particularly forgiveness of the self, but our failure to do so, lifetime after lifetime, is quite frankly why we have the problems, heartaches, disillusionment, illness and emotional baggage that we do. *The level of distress and anguish we experience in life is simply a measure of what we have failed to forgive.*

The real benefit of forgiveness is that it allows us to live our current life on a higher, clearer, and more joyous level, which is our strongest desire each time we return here. When PLT is viewed this way, it becomes not so much some esoteric, recreational pastime, as it does an avenue to greater insight, a tool with which to understand and reconstruct our lives, an opportunity to release ourselves from the confinement of personal pain, and an important step toward a more spiritually fulfilling existence.

In the chapters which follow, you will learn specifically how, through the PLT process, this occurred to me. During the months I was involved with the therapy process, and even more so in the years subsequent to that experience, I managed to finally break the stranglehold which feelings of low self-worth, powerlessness and futility had over my life. I put to rest all the disquiet, anger and abandonment I felt in my relationships with my parents, and actually *grew up*. I gained valuable skills and insights about myself and my loved ones, which still aid me in all my ongoing relationships. I learned at last to value myself and my talents, and to thank adversity for relentlessly showing me what is truly worthwhile about living in the here and now.

I developed the ability to hear the voice of my Higher self, to whom I can go at any moment—in the throes of any crisis—for guidance, and most importantly, the reassurance that I am never alone or without love. And last, but not least, the chain of events, spiritual insights and experiences which evolved out of my venturing into past-life regression helped build in me a sturdy, solid faith in the goodness and rightness of the Universe and all that happens within it.

Granted, the individual progress made within this journey was not due to past-life regression therapy alone, and I still feel myself to be at a point within some spiritual process which will ever continue to require daunting levels of self-honesty, dedication and work. But, as the expression goes, anything worth having is worth working for, and I find that where I am now is a *much* favorable place to where I stood before PLT.

It has been five years since my past-life regression therapy, and though my desire to further investigate my past lives has waned over time, I find that past-life experiences can still have impact in my life. This story is one that has shown itself to be continuing, and what follows is simply a record to-date of a journey, which has not yet realized its end.

Part One:

Aspects of Relationship

"Closing the Distance"

Chapter One

Closing the Distance

In the album of pictures I keep from my childhood, there is only one photograph of my father and me. It was taken after church one Sunday in 1955, shortly after our move to the new house he built for us that year, a modern, red brick ranch with five bedrooms.

The garage door stands open and gaping behind us, the lawn is still unseeded, and the cement for our front porch has not yet been poured. He is turned sideways toward me, holding me up in one of his big arms. Though the picture is out of focus, I can see he's not smiling. I am reaching up to adjust the band of my straw hat, my small face wearing the pinched look it always took on in the photographs of this period.

It is hard to imagine what the purpose of this picture might have been. At whose suggestion had it been taken? Perhaps it marked the first Easter Sunday in our new house: the carpenter and his youngest offspring. Perhaps it had been posed for only to placate the whim of an older sibling, who wished to try his hand at using the Brownie. Whatever the case, no one, including the blurry-faced child whose long thin legs dangle from her father's arm, could have guessed the significance it would one day assume. No one could have realized that this photograph would one day represent for her the only tangible piece of evidence that there once had been a relationship between this man and this child.

Until a few years ago, whenever I looked at this photograph, I used to think it held the secret of a love between my father and me, which had largely gone unexpressed. I imagined that if I stared hard enough into the eyes and hearts of those two blurry figures, the shot would suddenly jog into focus and reveal once and for all the source of the endless yearning I had always felt for this man, and the reason why something deep and obscure held us apart.

While I was growing up, I never questioned why my father seemed so distant from our family. It was the way fathers were in the fifties, before the social awareness and feminism of the sixties decreed that children needed fathers for more than financial support and occasional disciplinary action. In our household, my mother made the rules and set the structure of our domestic life. My father took on a sort of back-up role, as the enforcer of those rules. He would sit in his chair after work, reading the paper or watching the news, and occasionally, a volcanic "Stop!" would thunder forth from him, in the event we were getting too loud, or too sassy with our mother. Perhaps that's what made him so frightening, the sheer infrequency of him and the troubling unpredictability of that moment he would decide to explode into our world. It was a bit like being an offspring of Thor.

I know that the regrets I once felt about the lack of closeness I experienced with my father are not unusual. In fact, lately it has become rather commonplace for members of my generation to ponder the enrichment a more accessible and involved father might have brought to their lives. Still, I have to admit it does seem strange to me sometimes, when I look at modern-day fathers with their children, that my father never took me anywhere, not to a movie, or to the park, or even for a walk. There were so many of us at home, maybe it was unreasonable to have *ever* expected singular attention, but, for years it bothered me greatly that I had never known a sense of comfort with my father, only the sort of quiet and polite awkwardness that exists between perfect strangers.

Everything in the way of how we should act around him, how he felt about things, even the gifts we received for a birthday or Christmas, all came by way of our mother. The image I held of my father was never really in focus; that's why the lone picture I had of the two of us seemed somehow so accurate in its portrayal: a father with a bearing and expression which revealed nothing and a young child, seemingly distracted and fidgety from a proximity which never felt right to her.

***

And yet, there was no way I could not have known of the tenderness and sensitivity of the man who was my father. That part of him was actually quite transparent. When he was happy, he sang openly and loudly into the evening air of the kitchen, an odd assortment of favorites that never varied: *The Tennessee Waltz, The Autumn Leaves, Blueberry Hill*, and *You Don't Know Me*. He liked Mario Lanza and songs from *The Student Prince*, old Irish ballads and religious hymns, in particular the *Ave Maria*. He sang passionately and without self-consciousness, hitting the high notes in his soft, gravelly tenor, and whenever I reminisce about those moments and the sweet sincerity of that voice, even now, it makes me want to cry.

What was so hard to decipher were his silent moods, which, when they came, seemed to descend on the whole house like a vapor. We would never be able to determine what caused them, or what broke them. Days would pass and suddenly, the silly sense of humor, which I believe entertained *him* more than the rest of us, would return. "How about some lemonawdy?" he would boom, delighting in his curious insistence on the mispronunciation of certain words. Icy cream, sewerkraut, frenchy toast, the list went on. He spouted out new ones as he thought of them, and though we would respond with a practiced roll of our eyes, this would only amuse him further.

How could I have reconciled the disparity within this personality: the man who on one hand spent so much time withdrawn into the privacy of his own contagious gloom (for which I always felt somehow responsible), with the man who would open a package of underwear at Christmas and insist (mostly for the benefit of his children) on trying them, one after another, on his head, while we rolled on the floor with laughter? It always seemed that as we adjusted ourselves to one side of our father's personality or the other, its flip side would appear from out of nowhere. As my father's children, we learned the mercurial dance of mood swing, and how to shift our own behavior, automatically, to suit his, like the pupil of an eye fluctuating between stings of light and dark.

If it seemed we never got along much, my father and I, I don't think it was because we didn't want to. It was just that there wasn't much to build on, sharing as little as we did. I grew up in his space; we ate meals together with the others; he drove us to church every Sunday, and sat at the end of the pew, solemn and dignified, the fine sculpture of his cheekbones and jaw like something of the church itself. He would raise his voice in prayer and song—you could always pick it out from the rest of the congregation—and when the mass would close with *Holy God, We Praise Thy Name*, the sheer volume and passion of his singing would send chills up my spine.

It's not that there weren't *any* special moments between us. I seem to remember on Saturday nights, we enjoyed watching *Gunsmoke* together, eating our Jordan almonds and laughing at what my father called the cornball parts. "Well, Marshall," Chester would moralize at the end of an episode, "I reckon all that killin' wasn't over nothin' but a sack of taters," and my father and I would split our sides laughing.

I also remember a lot of summer evenings, when we sat on the front porch together, playing word games and making up songs. I could smell the deep, sticky fragrance of the honeysuckle bushes behind the house, and watch, as we sat, the silent explosion of fireflies, pulsing through the deep blue air. Those were the summers of the early sixties, when I was still a little girl, and that is about the time that my memories of those few close and gentle times with him stop.

As I entered my teenage years, what little connection I ever felt to this detached and complicated man was somehow completely lost, as I too, became complicated and detached. I began to question the value of the things on which my parents had built a life for me. The principles of the Catholic faith in which I had been raised and the relevance of my high school education gradually became more and more suspect. I grew to loathe the small town in which I had grown up, and a good deal of the people who lived there. In the end, my convictions on these topics became so strong, that I still feel as adamantly about them now as I did then.

For my mother, these changes were upsetting and perhaps a little embarrassing. But my father always took things more personally. My rebellion against the structure and tenets he had laid for me and my siblings was deeply hurtful and confusing. As I veered more and more from the careful path on which his own life was grounded, he became increasingly fretful for my well-being and future. Somehow the role which he had undertaken as my father, to ensure that I went out into the world with both feet planted firmly on the ground, was now being frustrated in a way for which he hadn't been prepared. "Now what?" he must have wondered to himself, as I left the house for school in braids and beads, suede-fringed shirts and tie-dyed pants.

"You," he would say, as I entered college and lounged about the kitchen table, expounding on abortion rights, male chauvinism, the ills of the Nixon administration, and, of course, the Vietnam War, "you've gone off the deep end." What had changed was that I no longer felt intellectually intimidated by him; I could see that he was fallible now, and began to take a sort of perverse delight in blowing cannonball-sized holes through his views on things.

What hadn't changed, though, was that underneath it all, it still broke my heart to disappoint him. I still longed for his wholehearted and unconditional approval, the way, I suppose, he longed for mine. Each wanted the other to turn and say, "You know, I've thought about what you said, and I believe you're right about this after all." Each of us would settle for nothing less, unable to accept the fact that being different substantiated the distance we had always suspected existed between us. We gave each other guarded looks across the kitchen table, which I believe by then had grown to a girth of about a thousand echoey feet.

One night, when I was in my early twenties, as my father drove me home to the apartment in which I lived at the time, he began to explain how he always believed that it was the woman's role to be with the children. He felt he wasn't supposed to invade the territory my mother had seemed to mark around us and herself. He allowed her to distance herself from him, as her time and energies became absorbed with childrearing, and, at the same time, sacrificed any closeness that might have developed between himself and his children, feeling as he did that women were better at things like that.

I never understood what prompted that strange confession from him. I also never realized until now what a revelation it was. Being young and self-involved, I didn't comprehend the tone of sadness and regret leaking out from inside of him, as he drove his big rattling car and stared ahead into the traffic. I hadn't picked up on the subtle apology he offered for the chasm that yawned between us and would never be bridged. I thought at the time that he was only defending the position he had taken in the family, though it now seems more like he was questioning the sanity of it, coming closer than perhaps he ever had to saying, "I should have tried harder to reach you; I should have leaned further across the table."

***

When my son was two years old, he played hide-and-seek by lying down in the center of a room with his eyes tightly shut. In his limited grasp of the world around him, he believed that as long as he couldn't *see* his playmates, they would never be able to find him.

When my father died fifteen years ago, I think my understanding of his death was somewhere on this level. In the initial stages of his passing, I was certain that because I couldn't see my father anymore, we would never be able to locate one another. He must be existing *somewhere*, I thought, but where exactly had he gone? Was he sailing around in outer space now, or what?

I found that the sudden nature of his departure—due to a ruptured aneurysm—had a very disorienting impact on me. His physical disappearance almost seemed like some peculiar optical illusion, as if he had gone off in a puff of smoke or become lodged under the false bottom of a Chinese box, the ongoing action of his life strangely frozen around the space he once occupied. It was difficult for me to sometimes understand why his things were all still around: the house he'd built, the suits he wore to church on Sunday, the strange flat pencils he used to mark wood.

Whenever I sat and looked at these things, I used to have the sense that their presence somehow ensured the return of his, that in the next moment he would come and take his seat at the desk across the room and begin rifling with his thick, weathered fingers through the stacks of papers there.

He would pick up his pen and begin making out a bill to one of his customers, and he would call to my mother in the kitchen, as he had a hundred times before: "How do you spell aluminum, love?"

At that point in my grief process, I simply longed to see what he looked like, and in what sort of place he was living. One night, I dreamt I found him in a large hall filled with people. He was playing the banjo and singing to a crowd that had gathered around him. He seemed happier than I ever remembered him, and there was a casualness in his manner I had never known. At his feet sat a small, smoky-colored dog, much like the dog my father had loved, and my mother had given away years before his death because it pee-ed once too often on her furniture.

The dream was troubling because it made me feel so anonymous to him: I had become a face just like any other in the crowd. But, it helped me to realize how weighted I still was with feeling for him, loaded down with all my unrequited love, like some sad refugee, who, having no where to put things, must carry everything that is meaningful to her. Now that he was dead, it didn't seem he'd have a use for my love anymore, just as he no longer needed the clothes, books, and tools he'd left behind.

In the months just after my father's death, I shuffled around the structure of my life until it became something completely different from the life my father had left. I quit graduate school, in which I was majoring in English, and went to New York City, where I moved in with my oldest sister and took a job at an insurance brokerage firm. I thought a lot less of the world once my father left it, and I guess that's why I shed as much as I could of the life I was living when he died.

Then one day, about a year after his death, as I was crossing Manhattan on my way home from work, it suddenly occurred to me that my father still loved me. It was a startling and charming concept, that *the dead* love back, and it struck me at that moment as so unbelievably logical, I couldn't understand why I hadn't realized it all along.

Suddenly, it seemed clear to me that the process of grief was not a retreat, but an act of pulling closer, an act of sharpening my perceptions and learning a new language, because my father spoke in signs now, and if I hadn't seen them before, it was because I had my eyes shut tight.

I realized it was I who had blocked the continuance of our relationship, because I hadn't trusted in the continuance of his spirit. I had confused the ending of his life on earth with the ending of his being and the bond that connected us. My father had simply changed form, and, who knew? Perhaps the love between us could grow lighter and stronger now, unburdened as it suddenly had become of all the qualifications we once placed upon it.

Several years later, while on a business trip in Paris, I was taken by an associate on a quick tour of the Louvre. As I hadn't much time before my plane, we decided it would be best to concentrate on just one area of interest. I have always liked the Impressionists, and while the collection there is limited, the two of us set off to locate it. I have little or no sense of direction and my guide didn't seem to have much more. It appeared that we kept circling round and ending up in the same place. As we entered one particular hall for our second dose of *déjà-vu*, I turned around in the opposite direction and was startled to see behind me a painting that had been a favorite of my father's. It was Georges de La Tour's *Saint Joseph Charpentier*, a beautiful rendering of the child Jesus, holding up a candle for St. Joseph the Carpenter, at work in his shop. I had given my father a reprint of this picture for Christmas one year.

The painting was larger and more imposing than I had imagined. It had a certain presence that made me feel weightless by comparison. I stood, suspended in front of it, as if held by string, until my companion touched my arm.

I tried to explain the significance of this startling occurrence. I gestured at the picture and smiled numbly at her through tearing eyes. "It's too bad he couldn't have been here with you to see it," she said, sympathetically. I looked at her and nodded, realizing there were no words to convincingly relay the fact that it was my dead father who had steered me there in the first place. For a few moments, it seemed, we lingered on, my father, my friend and me, and finally I understood something he'd been trying to tell me all along. My father, though dead, had left *nothing* of his life behind him, not his memories, not the things he loved and certainly not me.

Though he never played the banjo in his lifetime, that is how I came to think of my father, sitting in that vast hall, so cheerful and relaxed. I tried to imagine that his new existence was something like one long, sustained perfect moment, free from all the worry and isolation in which he seemed to live half his life. I liked to believe he still told the same jokes and still sang *The Tennessee Waltz*, and that he was appreciated there—wherever that was—for his warmth and sensitivity.

***

Even though, in the years following his death, I'd come to trust in the faithful presence of my father's spirit in my life, conversations were still never easy-going. The table where we now sat down to talk had assumed celestial proportions, and it always took a long time for the answers to come back.

The gap between us still felt echoey and big. There was consolation in the understanding that he wasn't gone completely, but in reality, he didn't seem anymore there than he ever had been, and our ill-fitting connection to one another often felt as disabled and hopeless as it always had.

In the final analysis, I felt I'd been nothing but a problem to him. As the years passed and I no longer needed to question and rebel purely for its own sake, I began to feel guilty about the way I *had* acted. Gradually, my behavior towards him in the last years of his life grew to seem completely unconscionable. What had I been thinking?

My father had raised enough children to understand the normal separation process that maturing children go through with their parents, a necessary process, really, which a wise parent tries to overlook and ride out for the sake of his child's maturation and coming of age. A few years pass, and the child's need to disconnect passes with it. Unfortunately, my father left before this seemingly harmless and inevitable process reached resolution. Sometimes, I thought he must have given up waiting, assuming I was too far gone to ever feel inclined to make the circle back. Apparently, he thought the homing device had gone a bit haywire with his last child.

So, why couldn't he have stuck it out, I thought? Did I seem so hopelessly irretrievable to him that he couldn't trust in the power of instinct and the passage of time to compel me back someday within a range shorter than shouting distance?

Years would pass when I gave up acknowledging his spirit completely, caught up in one of my sticky patches of anger at him for having never taken proper care of me in the first place. I felt, well, he had his own work to do now, and I had mine, this business of growing up and getting on with things.

But your mind has a way of making pronouncements that your heart has no means of embracing. Through all my philosophizing, through all my spiritual and intellectual understanding of his death, through all my attempted acceptance of his absence from my life, I still felt little more than regret and a deep, unshakeable sadness where my father and I were concerned. I longed still, as I had always longed, for the relationship which had never blossomed and now had no hope of ever coming to pass.

***

I entered past-life regression therapy in January of 1990, close to eleven years after my father's death. I didn't go to work right away on my relationship with him, but knew from the beginning it was something I wanted to clear and understand better. Specifically, I wanted to resolve my childhood feelings of abandonment by him, something that his death had exacerbated, and more importantly, to get rid of the anger that brewed up from inside of those feelings and continued to ensure a guarded distance between us.

Five weeks into my therapy, I asked for insight into the past-life history I had to my feelings of abandonment with my father. It was interesting to me that the lifetime which appeared in response to that question was not one that I shared with my father at all, but a recreation of the abandonment issue in more dramatic form with another important male figure from my present life—my older brother, Bracken.

It led me to understand that our karmic connections to others do not have to be replayed in some literal format. We can solve or agree to work on old issues—like abandonment—with new players and under new circumstances. Resolution, if achieved, is every bit as complete and purifying as if that score had been settled with the original co-creator of the issue, in this case, my brother.

It seems that shortly before the turn of this century, I was born into a wealthy English family, and lived on an estate somewhere in Cheshire. At about the age of fifteen, I was thrown from a horse and paralyzed from the waist down. My own unwillingness to deal with this disability, and more importantly, what I perceived to be my father's rejection of me because of it, resulted in a rather rash move, which brought about my own suicide at the age of about sixteen.

(This transcript represents the **second** time I had uncovered this particular lifetime. The year is about 1910.)

J: This has something to do with a horse. I'm not on the horse. This could be from my lifetime in England, because the person I see on the horse is my brother Bracken, who was my father in that lifetime. I see him there on the horse, and I think I'm on the ground. His horse is rearing up, but it's not out of control. He may have just ridden up; maybe I was lying on the ground and he came back to see what was going on. I'm on the ground on my side.

M: What happens next?

J: He's trying to see what's wrong with my back. He's putting his hand there and I'm flinching. There's another horse there.

M: Have you fallen from the horse?

J: Yes.

M: How did that happen?

J: I fell off and I was kicked by the horse. The horse reared up and struck me on the back.

M: Go to the next significant part. (Hereafter NSP.)

J: There are some men who have come out from the house. They work on the estate, and they've come to move me. They have a stretcher made out of branches and something like a black oilcloth. They move me onto it, and it's very painful.

M: NSP.

J: There's an old black car. It's like a van or a sedan-type car. It must be like an ambulance or something. I guess I'm being taken to a hospital.

M: NSP.

J: We're in some kind of hospital. My father is very anxious, and he's yelling at the people around him to get with it.

M: NSP.

J: I'm in a hospital bed. I'm lying flat.

M: What is your name in this life?

J: Margaret Kendall.

M: Okay, Margaret, tell me what happens next.

J: I'm in a wheel chair at home and I'm yelling at someone who's supposed to be taking care of me. I'm saying I want her discharged, and to get her away from me. There's a pan of water on the floor that I've knocked over in my rage.

M: NSP.

J: There's some discussion going on between my father and this woman who is my stepmother. They don't know I've come into the room. I'm in my wheelchair and their backs are toward me. She feels that they have to do something about me, because I'm out of control and angry all the time. She feels they need to look into the situation to see if there's anything that can be done, and I guess that if there isn't anything that can be done physically to remedy the situation, then she feels I should be put into a home somewhere and taken care of there.

M: What does your father think?

J: He doesn't know what to do, but he's very much under her control because he's so unsure of what is the right thing to do. He becomes swayed by her because she seems to be so unemotional and clear-headed about the whole thing.

M: So, what's the result?

J: I'm getting sent to a clinic of some sort. I'm getting bundled up in blankets. I have a cape on. I can see the front of the house. There's a great big circular drive. I'm with a woman who's like a governess. My father and stepmother aren't with me. I'm real angry about my stepmother. I feel that she's just trying to ease me out of the picture, and she's just using this as an excuse. I feel, it's enough that I have this physical problem, and then she's sort of using it to get me out of the way.

M: NSP.

J: I'm in the hospital again. I'm being examined. They're going to operate. They think that there are bone fragments causing the problem. They hope to remove the fragments that are blocking the brain messages to my legs.

M: NSP.

J: The surgery was exploratory. They had no way of knowing what the damage was really like. They were just hoping that it wasn't really crushed, that there were a few bone fragments that could be removed. But when they operated, they found just a mass of crushed bone.

M: They weren't able to straighten it out then?

J: No.

M: What happens next?

J: Well, I guess I'm going to end up being put in a home, and I'm really angry at my father because he's agreeing to this. He seems to feel that they're not able to give me adequate care, and he's very concerned about me. He has some illusion that if I'm sent away to a hospital or a professional place that they'll be able to fix me up mentally and make me into a good invalid.

M: NSP.

J: I'm outside in my wheel chair. My father's with me. I think I'm supposed to be leaving the next day for that place. It's Sunday. My father has wheeled me to the top of this hill, and I've told him I just want to sit there for a while and look at the view. He's gone down to check on something. One of the sheep that's caught in the fence or something we saw along the way. I'm really furious with him. I've decided to take matters into my own hands. I don't really feel that life is worth living, anyway, because not only am I an invalid, but I'm being sent to this institution to live, and so everything's being taken away from me. There doesn't seem to be any point in continuing on.

M: Do you feel abandoned by your father?

J: Yes. I'm angry at my stepmother, but I'm really angry at him. My stepmother doesn't have the connection to me that he does, and so in some ways I can see why she feels as she does. But I can't even believe he's for real.

M: So you feel abandoned by him?

J: It's like he feels I'm a hopeless case. The other part of it is that I just think he's acting so ineptly. He's being swayed along by everything my stepmother is saying, and that he isn't thinking for himself. He's really out of touch with his feelings and going along with the tide. And I'm the one who's losing.

M: Say how you feel.

J: *I just don't understand why he can't take care of me, because I would take care of him. He isn't thinking about how I feel. He's making a practical decision.*

M: *Is there anything else you're aware of feeling at this moment?*

J: *I think that by committing suicide* (I rolled myself down the hill in my chair and broke my neck.), *I not only take control of the situation, but I beat him to the punch. It's like before he can abandon me, I leave first.*

M: *Can you go to the moment of your death now?*

J: *Yes.*

M: *Can you go to where you see the light and ask your Higher self or one of the masters what further lessons do you need to learn from that life that would be helpful to you in this life. I'll count to five. (1-2-3-4-5.)*

J: *It's my father* (i.e., current life). *He says, "Let go of that anger. It doesn't matter anymore."*

M: *Ask if there's any other lessons you're to learn from that life.*

J: *He says, "When we were together, no one could have loved you more than I did."*

M: *What do you want to tell your father?*

J: *How much I miss him.*

M: *Talk to him now, and tell him. Ask him if there's any other lesson you need to learn.*

J: *He says, "Your father loved you then, your father loves you now."*

M: *Any other message?*

J: *He says, "I'm always here for you, and you're still my little girl."*

M: *What do you tell him?*

J: *That I love him.*

M: Tell him that you have to go, and that you'll see him again. Can you forgive your father in that life and your stepmother for any pain they may have caused you?

J: Yes.

M: Can you forgive yourself for the way you acted?

J: Yes.

M: Then, it's time to come back.

***

I came away from this regression experiencing a number of different insights and breakthroughs. Some were immediate; others have manifested more quietly over time. What struck me the most, initially, startled me in fact, was the sense of just how much my father had *wanted* to talk to me, and that his eagerness was not borne out of death, but had been there all along.

It got me thinking more about relationships in general, and how so often particular circumstances or dynamics within a relationship do more to define who the players are than their actual personalities or the potential within those personalities.

In each life, certain aspects of ourselves might be accentuated, while others are not, much like a figure in relief. Apparently, the part of my father that wished to communicate with me was really always there somewhere. Though he did not know how to express his feelings to me, if I think about it, I'm certain I always knew how deeply he wanted to. He had about him something like the strength of a good piece of literature, which tells more by what it doesn't say.

Past-life regression therapy opened up a channel between my father and me. It broke down all the barriers and misapprehensions that had existed previously for me. This particular session was not the only time he appeared and spoke to me about my lives past and present. I found that after communicating via the PLT sessions where he played an active role, it was easier for me to hear him even when I wasn't regressed.

Though I have on occasion, in recent years, through *clairaudience*, received information of all sorts from many different spiritual sources, my own father's voice has always been the clearest and strongest of them all. I have never been in doubt that it was him there, nor has there ever been a moment of vagueness about what he intended to say or how he wanted it said, the clarity and power of his voice apparently unaltered from those Sunday mornings in church when he used to shake the rafters with his singing.

Another realization which hit me soon after this PLT session was exactly what significance the life of Margaret held for me, and why this incarnation perhaps rather than any other had been chosen by my unconscious mind. It seemed that my prior life experience as Margaret left me with some residual anger and fear of paternal abandonment. By the time I reached 15 or so years of age, (the point at which Margaret began to doubt her own father's loyalty), this anxiety of abandonment, with which I came into life, intensified, and I began, for the sake of my own self-preservation, to draw myself inexplicably away from my father.

My father was no more equipped to deal with my anger and rejection of him than Margaret's father had been capable of handling *hers*, and so he did the one thing which he always did whenever he felt conflict arise between himself and someone he loved—he shut down. As I felt him fade, my anger intensified, and in his confusion, he endeavored to disappear completely. His death, of course, was his ultimate gesture of withdrawal from my life. It left me stunned and short-circuited, the way you feel when someone walks out on an argument you believe yourself to be winning. "Okay, now what?" I wanted to say, looking around me at an emptiness as intense as his presence had once been.

What I didn't understand then, and what past-life regression therapy helped me to learn is that the bond between two individuals continues from lifetime into death, from lifetime to lifetime, through emotional trauma and pain of *all* sorts, through all the devastating hurt that humans seem ever more capable of heaping on themselves and each other. And through it all, the bond is not damaged or compromised, but simply made stronger.

Granted there is overlap and repetition of old issues and power struggles: anxieties, jealousies, resentments, and fears, but ultimately, the particular failure of a given relationship is not the point at all. We don't choose our relationships because of what they have been in the past, but for what they can teach us going forward, and the potential to grow and learn within the confines of any and all relationships—whether or not we actually succeed in doing so—is unlimited.

A lot of what we long for when we come into life is simply to be together—to be—and at that point we don't place the kinds of values or expectations on that experience as we do once we're in it. As evolving souls—and all of us are that—we have this unflagging hope that in our new lives, relationships and experiences, we will finally acquire a level of tolerance, forgiveness, and unconditional love that we've promised ourselves all along.

I am now more aware of the depth of my father's love, and any longing I once had for what was or might have been is gone. I spend no more time or energy on regret, guilt, blame, anger or disappointment. Instead I accept wholeheartedly the father he was and the daughter I have been to him. Over time, in fact, I have come to see how perfectly engineered our relationship was and how it enabled and prompted me to work on and absolve century-old baggage.

It's true that my father left his life before our relationship achieved surer footing. But it's clear now that that was never important. Valuable lessons and insights came to me through the experience of his death and his after-life, a different sort of knowledge of love and life I could not have garnered elsewhere, and would probably not have been motivated to acquire, if the loss of him had not been so alarming.

***

The process of past-life regression, though utterly profound and life-altering, is actually quite subtle in its method, delivering its impact in a sort of short-handed or even understated way. It is hard for me to convey sometimes, when I look back at certain transcripts or think back on certain moments during the experience, just how powerful some messages or incidents were to me. The therapy itself, I have found, has a two-pronged curative affect on your life, one which is immediate and cathartic, the other which sort of distills and unravels itself silently over time.

The source of the power in past-life material is I think a little like the process of reduction in cooking. By allowing a broth or flavored liquid to boil down to a smaller, condensed amount, a chef will create a sauce more potent in flavor. This phenomenon seems true of the stuff regressions are made of; broad sweeping issues that seem all-consuming and all-pervasive in present-day life, are suddenly brought down to a size and shape which is visual, comprehensible and manageable. The insight and perspective that this distilled format brings with it is utterly potent in its effect.

We develop a kind of tunnel vision throughout the course of day-to-day life, seeing only ourselves and our problems. Because of this limited perspective, we are not aware of alternative perspectives or even the true insignificance of issues we believe to be insurmountable. Nor do we see how enduring and powerful we are as entities. Consider that after all the situations, trials, tribulations and even deaths we've experienced across time, we've always come back! We've always been given another chance, another body, another life, brand new relationships, opportunities and potential. This is not to say, go ahead and waste the life you've been given here, who cares? It's to say, don't fret about the sorrows, because nothing in life is ever truly lost.

Though past-life regression opens up a window to the past, it does not encourage one to dwell on the past. Instead, it seems to break down the limitations we place upon our present life and demonstrate the unlimited potential of each moment. It seems to shift the focus away from the failures of the past to the promise of the future, urging us to climb as high as we desire to go. It teaches us, in fact, that failure is an illusion.

I learned, for instance, that the failure I once saw in my relationship with my father, that he couldn't care for me and had left me to deal with my own problems, was utterly false. My father stuck by me after his death until I reached a point in my own spiritual development where I no longer needed to rely on his help. At that point I freely and happily let him go. What he said to me during the regression enclosed in this chapter was really true: "no one could have loved me more than (he) did."

I have come, in fact, to a place in my assessment of that relationship, where I see it as a prototype for all my other relationships. Whenever I have trouble with any other person in my life, and I despair about the outcome of particular problems or dynamics, I look for reassurance at how far my father and I progressed, and what a calm, comfortable place we ultimately reached.

It doesn't matter to me that my father never took me out for ice cream; it doesn't even matter that he no longer lives on this earth. To us, our relationship is a living, present and perfect thing. And we value it just the way it is.

***

Life is a spectacular evolution. Yet, somehow, we fail to see the beauty of its progression. We continue to take our snapshots of life, and try to hold moments static, but time rolls ever away, and the day comes when the once important loses meaning. We look back to find people who no longer exist in the form in which they appear, wearing clothes that are hopelessly out of fashion, and expressions of care and interest in things which are no longer relevant.

I suppose the only thing which does endure, which does remain constant is the bond itself, that thing I used to look for whenever I squinted into the pinched face of myself at three, cradled high in the arm of the man who was my father. But something so fluid and timeless cannot be reflected in a thing which is, by nature, a limited medium. A photograph is only capable of revealing that there once was a man and a child who stood together on a space of newly developed land on a certain Sunday in 1955. What explains the significance of the relationship between them is quite invisible to the naked eye. It cannot be sought after in pictures or even in words. It can only be found here, under the heart, where all love is memorized, perfectly preserved and eternal.

"A Lesson in Sorrow"

Chapter Two

A Lesson in Sorrow

My mother loved music. She sang frequently and well, with a crystal clear, operatic soprano that spiralled gracefully up the scales, and even if you had been blessed enough to hear it everyday of your life, it could still give you pause. It could circle to heights you wouldn't think a human voice even dared, (especially since she could peel potatoes at the same time), but soar it did, that voice of hers, so far up into the blue sometimes, you had the feeling you were hearing a sound that belonged only in heaven.

Perhaps it was only natural, then, that it was her music which changed first, heralding for us—if we had only understood the sign—the strange and rocky waters through which we would all ride out the last five years of her life.

At the age of seventy-three, my mother, whose lifestyle, personality and tastes had remained fairly constant for as long as we, her children, could remember, suddenly became a fan of Country-Western music. It amused us, I have to say, since it seemed somewhat uncharacteristic for a woman whose music interests had never ventured much beyond "easy listening" and songs from the war era.

When she came to my home in Connecticut for a visit in the summer of 1990, I found her spending most of her waking hours in front of my TV, totally hooked on the cable station from Nashville. From time to time, she would call me in from the other room to hear particular songs she liked or to introduce me to the singing stars who now filled up her life.

I remember that it was interesting to watch my mother change, even in this insignificant way, to allow her—as I tried a little middle-aged maturity on for size—some measure of ordinary personhood, when at heart I rarely ever thought of her as a real person. As an adult, I had tried to give my mother latitude. I had endeavored to know, understand and even like her as a person, though I had rarely been successful.

I had also struggled to make her know and appreciate me. And, admittedly, I had been disappointed many times over because her behavior had persistently demonstrated that the person she believed me to be was no more real than the woman I saw when I looked at her.

I guess that made me no different than any other child who ever walked the earth. And I guess my mother was no different than any other parent who ever had a child that expected her to remain true to an image which didn't favor change.

One day that summer while riding in the car, she discovered a Country-Western tape of mine and asked me to play it for her. Once the music picked up its honky-tonk beat, she began nodding her head and slapping her knee in this rather odd portrayal of a woman who is carefree and light of heart.

I couldn't believe how strange she seemed to me in that moment, as if her body had suddenly been overtaken by some hill-spirit from Tennessee. What seemed so odd to me, though, wasn't the newfound taste for Country-Western music, but her unusual show of lightheartedness, this seemingly frenzied attempt to convince herself with each tap of her knee, that life was free and easy, with no more intricacy and sadness than the familiar cadence of the tune she was humming.

My mother had always been a woman who found it difficult to enjoy herself, and I couldn't for the life of me figure out from where this demonstration of gaiety sprang. Though she never talked about her childhood, my five siblings and I always suspected this to be the source of her unrelenting disenchantment with life. She was born the second child of eleven to poor Irish parents, a circumstance which I believe always secretly appalled her. It was as if she'd come into life expecting more, and could never quite forgive her family or her life for being so ordinary.

However, as a young woman, she *was* exceptionally beautiful. Perhaps she felt it was the one blessing that had come her way. Her looks drew attention from outsiders that she never received at home (she was crowned the May Queen of our church at the age of twenty-one), and that became, I believe she felt, her ticket to something better. Unfortunately, thereafter, physical attractiveness became the one criterion on which she evaluated herself and everybody else, that being the only arena in which she felt prepared to compete.

With each passing year, as her natural beauty waned, her sense of security also began to slip. Her tolerance under adversity virtually crumbled in later years, particularly after the death of my father. There was after all, no inner strength to shore her up, and as time went on, her reactions to the tragic events of her life—the death of her oldest son, the loss of her youngest sister to Alzheimer's disease—never progressed beyond a stage of complete and abject shock. It was as if she got lodged on the crest of the initial wave of those events, repeating the story over and over again to anyone who would listen, as if the re-telling would suddenly make it explicable or somehow acceptable.

While my mother couldn't seem to ever lean into the tragic turns in the road of her life, she was, in a way, quite at home with the morbidity with which she infused her existence here. It was not unusual in the last years of her life when you took her out somewhere, to look up suddenly and find her across the room, embroiled in the act of cornering some unsuspecting stranger, pressing into their reluctant and embarrassed hands a copy of my brother's death notice (which she had laminated), the eulogy which I wrote for him, or pictures of his children.

She made us angry with this behavior. We were ashamed and frustrated, unable to figure out why she couldn't just get beyond things and carry on with her life. But this *was* her life, in a way, this strange, never-ending jag of sorrow. "No one knows what I'm going through," she would say to us again and again. "Yes," we would think, "least of all, you."

It is one of life's paradoxes that we often elicit from others the very response we fear. So it was that my mother, in seeking the attention she had always craved, would browse through the main street of the town where we grew up, poking in and out of shops and restaurants, replete with family memorabilia and well-worn anecdotes of sick and dying loved ones—for anyone who would listen. The response of the people in the town and the members of her family had been to retreat—at varying speeds—once they became convinced that no amount of indulgence or understanding or consolation could eradicate this vibrant morosity of hers, a morosity that could flatten from fifty paces any ounce of optimism you had ever carried inside your being.

Oddly enough, this unfortunate turn of events speaks more to me of my mother's power than of anything else. It was not just the contagious effects of her bleak view of life which struck me as evidence of her power, but the endlessness of the search we, as her children, continued to make on her behalf, this odyssey for a prize that would always elude us, the thing which we were completely incapable of ever giving her, and that which she always had the power to make us spin cartwheels in order to produce—her happiness.

I realize it's not uncommon for a child to feel responsible for procuring a parent's happiness. With my mother, however, it was a bit more complicated than that. We grew up seeing the strain and anger at how her life had shaken out, and indeed felt responsible for remedying that. But there was never any signal from her as to what the antidote might be. She had no clue herself, having always been miraculously out of touch with herself, and even if she had, expressing one's needs requires a certain sense of self-deserving which my mother never owned.

There *was* a time when none of us had tired yet of the guessing, when none of us had completely sickened of the disappointment that came when our efforts to please elicited no response from her. But, I believe in the end the strength of my mother's commitment to remain lonely and unhappy even had the power to madden her. It changed her into someone we didn't know, and the experience of watching her grow more and more unreachable finally matured us as her children. In the end, you learn, it's not just the parent who struggles to let go.

Fifteen years ago, my mother's family held a reunion in New Haven, Connecticut. One night during the festivities, a thunderstorm blew up unexpectedly, and the majority of my relatives and I rushed indoors to safety. My mother and a few of her brothers and sisters, however, remained under a tent in the storm, reluctant to end the singing that engrossed them, until suddenly the weight of the water collecting in the folds of the tent's roof sent it crashing down on their heads. My mother approached the door to the house, soaking wet and absolutely paralyzed with laughter. When I went out to retrieve her, she started to tell me what had happened, but her laughter rendered her speechless and limp in my arms. I had never seen her laugh like that. She came into the bright kitchen, all animated and giggly, with the tears of her laughter spilling unbounded down her beautiful face.

For all the years afterward and up to the time of her death, I thought about that moment and the woman she had been then. But, the image for me was always foreign and haunting; foreign because it was the face of someone I never knew, haunting because, somewhere underneath my decision to simply allow her to be who she was, I knew I still hoped—the way I had hoped as a child—to be the one to find that woman for my mother—and introduce the two of them.

***

I was the last of my mother's children. There were five others ahead of me, at the time of my birth, ages twelve through five. When I arrived on the scene, children were anything but a novelty for my mother, who would tell you it had never been her decision to have so many children, so close together. One wonders where she was when the conceiving took place, but it was her contention that the size and design of the family were somehow shaped by the whim of my father and, I guess, the edicts of the Catholic Church, which did not permit the use of birth control.

This rather non-committal posturing which my mother freely put forth on the matter of our pro-creation, tended to make my siblings and me feel a bit like unexpected house guests. But as a child, I could only assume that her boredom with me had something to do with my inability to charm. I struggled for years, as both a child and an adult, to attract her attention. But, she just didn't seem to have the natural inclination, which normal parents have, to care about the achievements, the disappointments or changes in my life. She was always vague on the details, whether I was still in graduate school, what degree I was taking, where I worked, what I did there, how I spent my time, what mattered to me. In the last two minutes of an hour-and-a-half long-distance call, she would inquire on the status of things—was I still in school, what was that degree called, how was my roommate—before signing off. But, there was no support, encouragement, praise or interest in the things that mattered completely to me. Not ever.

Most of us are familiar with the feelings of sadness and anger that descend in adult life once you begin to recognize that your parent's treatment of you as a child was somehow wanton. It is regrettable that many of my contemporaries have come to view their own childhoods from the perspective of how damaged they were when they emerged, and how much they have had to struggle throughout adult life to eradicate those effects.

For many years, it was still possible for me to make excuses for my mother. I used to say that she found it hard to be interested in my life because there was no overlap with hers. After all, she had never attended college, lived away from home, or gone on a business trip. With marriage and children, there was more familiar territory, I thought. Until one summer, during a visit to my home, when I endeavored to explain to her the difficulties we'd had with my son during his first years of life. (He had three operations before the age of two.) Her vision wandered around the kitchen for a few moments as I talked, and then it settled on the back of a cereal box, which she picked up and began to read.

It was then I learned that this woman, who spent every waking moment engaged in advancing her own emotional plight into a matter of public interest, was unable to absorb on any level the troubled patches in the lives of her children. With so much emotion invested in her own turmoil, there was simply no capacity left over for others, significant or otherwise.

In her later years, more than ever, conversation with her became completely one-sided. She had a variety of subjects on which she would ramble: my brother's death, people who gave her a "hard time," her increasing incapability to manage money, her loneliness, her lack of appetite, her insomnia. "I guess you've heard about how bad I've been lately," she would begin, laughing the odd laugh that foreshadowed the distressing monologue which was about to follow. Sometimes, I would respond, but mostly I just listened. It was clear to me she didn't want advice, or explanation, or even concurrence. She just wanted to talk.

I would drive the car and listen, as if tuned into some radio talk show where the host had lost control of the caller. I would watch the other cars on the road, glance back at my son, slumped over in his car seat, asleep, and wonder to myself, "How did she ever get this crazy? When did it all start? Is it just some gross exaggeration of the woman she's always been—self-absorbed, insensitive, overbearing at times—or are these new eccentricities, brought on by old age and loneliness? What do we do with her now," I would say to myself, "now that no one can stand to be around her?"

It was not possible for my mother, who had always been the most judgmental and intolerant person I knew, to grasp the irony of how so many others—family and friends—now found her company unbearable. What occurred to me then as I looked at her situation was how utterly embarrassed she would have been if she could have seen herself this way ten years before. Underneath, she was the last person, who would ever be able to forgive herself for the way she behaved in the last years of her life. Ten years ago, if she had seen the woman she was to become approaching her on the street, she would have crossed over to the other side, and ducked into a shop.

***

When I entered past-life therapy—four years before my mother's death—and began investigating my past lives, mothers like my mother became a noticeable pattern. There were two, in fact—one in my life on a farm in 19th century France and one in 18th century Amsterdam—who treated me with such contempt that for the first few minutes of the regression, I believed I was a servant rather than a daughter. But these past-life recalls helped me to understand why I had chosen my present mother to raise me in this lifetime. It was more my inward desire to break the pattern, rather than a perverse need to perpetuate it.

It seems to me that, coming in, we choose to continue difficulties we have faced before in order to give ourselves the opportunity to resolve and forgive the past, to end the destructive cycle, and move on. A lot of us, though, tend to resist the karmic work we initially set out to do, and instead, endure entire lifetimes of the emotional pain that repetitive, negative patterns will bring us.

With me, I went from many years of feeling that the unfortunate relationship I had with my mother was my fault, for being so thoroughly inadequate, to a number of years of feeling it was her fault, for much the same reason. I even told her so in a letter, in an effort to rid myself, once and for all, of my anger and disappointment at the lack of interest she had shown in me. It didn't work, though; my anger and disappointment survived.

My mother reacted, not with sympathy, or an attempt to understand my point of view, but with indignation and confusion. She circulated the letter throughout the family, and read it aloud to my brothers and sisters, in a tone of complete amazement, fully expecting them to join with her in her outrage. But they recognized the feelings expressed in that letter as ones of their own. It seemed to us the only attention we'd ever been given came by way of her criticism: the hair that was too curly, or the posture that was poor, the body which was too skinny, or the features garnered from our father. Why did she always seem to evaluate us in terms of what was wrong?

"She's only ever been able to see the empty half of the glass," my mother's sister said to me when I asked her this. Apparently, life had *always* fallen short for my mother. It didn't start with us. Perhaps, it was really an imperfect view of *herself* that prevented her from imagining that the children she brought into the world might be perfectly wonderful just the way they were.

By the time I entered past-life regression therapy, my anger with my mother was at an all-time high. It had gotten so big, I couldn't contain it at times, and once or twice, the rage that used to spill out of me during her annual visits had alarmed the hell out of me.

I used to tell my therapist, Marion, that my mother's overwhelming presence in my life felt like possession. "I sit and write something," I would say, "and it sounds great. A day or two later I look at it, and this voice says, 'what do *you* know about this?' Those words are my mother's, which I speak on her behalf. My mother's negative influence on me is the drop of lemon juice in the cup of milk. It will instantly sour everything."

I felt that because I had been raised without encouragement and reinforcement, I would always be destined to look skeptically at the things I accomplished. They would never be quite right, or good enough, because they had never been appreciated by the one person I had sought hardest to win over—my mother.

***

Asking the question which had plagued me most of my adult life—Why can't I let go of the anger I have for my mother?—I was regressed to a lifetime in the thirteenth century (part of which is excerpted below), where my mother and I lived together as brother and sister in an area of Europe, which had been settled by the Slavs. Her name was Greta and mine Enrich. Our mother died when Greta—who was born deformed and mentally retarded—was still a baby. We lived with our father (who is my brother Bracken in this life) in a small cabin high in the mountains, where my father and I made a living as fur trappers:

J: I'm going down a very steep hill covered with snow. It's very steep; it's taking me a long time to get down.

M: Are you by yourself?

J: Yes.

M: Why are you going down the hill?

J: I'm looking for something.

M: What is it?

J: I'm looking for my father.

M: Go to the next significant part. (Hereafter NSP.)

J: I'm by a cliff. It's very snowy. I've been out for a long time. I'm cold. I'm beginning to feel very hopeless; I've come to a dead end. I have to turn around and go back; I can't go any further in this direction.

M: NSP.

J: Something has been pulled like a chain or a clamp. I don't understand what this is about. I think my father got his foot caught in a trap.

M: Are you pulling your father?

J: No, it seems like I'm looking at the tracks where he dragged himself. There's blood in the snow.

M: Is your father still alive?

J: No, he's frozen to death.

M: How do you feel about that?

J: I'm horrified. The way he has died is very grotesque. His eyes are open, and his face is all frozen over. It looks like he was trying to crawl up the hill on his arm, and he got frozen in position. This person is my brother Bracken.

M: NSP.

J: I'm sitting with Greta.

M: What are you doing?

J: I'm trying to explain to her about our father dying.

M: What are you explaining, how he died?

J: It seems she's retarded or something, and I have to keep explaining it to her, as if she were a child. It's very heartbreaking, because she just can't quite grasp what has happened. She keeps smiling up into my face. Then, I explain it again.

M: Is your mother in that life dead?

J: Yes, I think so.

M: So just the two of you are left in that family?

J: Yes.

M: What do you plan to do?

J: Well, we'll stay there and I'll take care of her. She does all the housework and cooks and everything. I can still do the trapping.

M: How do the two of you get along?

J: We get along okay.

M: NSP.

J: I think it might be summer now. There doesn't seem to be any snow around. I guess I've been fishing. There are some streams in the mountains. I trap in the winter and fish in the summer. I have some fish with me, and I'm walking up the hill to where we live. It's a very small house.

M: NSP.

J: My sister's made me a shirt. It's badly made, but she's very proud of it.

M: What do you do?

J: I give her a hug, but I feel very sad.

M: For her or for you?

J: For her. She tries so hard and means so well, but she isn't capable of doing very much.

M: Is your sister younger or older than you?

J: Younger. She's about 18.

M: Are you sad for yourself, too?

J: I don't feel like I am. She's very easy to please. I mean, it's a simple existence but I don't expect much else. We live in a very plentiful area. We always have plenty to eat. The weather's very harsh, but we know how to live here. We can always get along.

M: You're 23 years old. Don't you ever think of getting yourself a wife?

J: No, I don't feel that way. I don't feel she's a burden or that I'm missing out.

M: You're not interested in any of the women in your village?

J: We live in a very isolated area. It's difficult to marry if you don't make special arrangements for that.

M: What kind of arrangements?

J: You have to go to the village and send a letter. I guess what you do then is post an ad. If there's a woman who wants to marry, and come and live in the mountains, she'll come and do that.

M: You haven't met such a woman?

J: No, I don't have any plans of doing that.

M: Is that because you're not interested or because you feel responsible for your sister?

J: I'm happy staying here with Greta.

M: NSP.

J: It's winter again. Greta seems to be sick.

M: What does she have?

J: She has a high fever.

M: Who takes care of her?

J: I've just come home and found her sick.

M: What do you do?

J: I'm giving her some broth.

M: What's it made from?

J: Rabbit.

M: NSP.

J: She's died. I don't know what was wrong with her. I think it was a virus she caught from an animal.

M: *How old are you now?*

J: *30, 33. I'm still in the cabin. It's very lonely. When I come home, it's cold in the cabin because there's no one there to keep the fire going.*

M: *What do you decide to do?*

J: *I don't decide to do anything. Life just goes on. I miss my sister. It's like losing a child.*

M: *NSP.*

J: *I'm just outside my house. I have a trap that goes into the stream to catch fish. I'm taking it out. There aren't a lot of fish. Either it's not a good season or I don't make the effort I used to. It's easier to just put the trap outside the house than to go all the way downstream where there's more fish.*

M: *NSP.*

J: *I'm riding a horse.*

M: *Where are you going?*

J: *To the village.*

M: *What are you going to the village for?*

J: *To get supplies.*

M: *How do you pay for the goods?*

J: *I have some pelts.*

M: *Do you see anyone when you go to the village?*

J: *No.*

M: *Is there someone at the store that you see?*

J: *There's a man I trade with there.*

M: Is he the only person you see?

J: Usually.

M: NSP.

J: I'm home again. I'm taking the horse around to the back.

M: Can you move ahead five years in that life and see what you come to?

J: It's dark. I'm just in the cabin alone.

M: Are you still lonely?

J: I guess so.

M: I want you to go ahead to the moment of your death, and tell me what's happening.

J: I've met up with a bear. He has me cornered on a hillside. He's struck me on the side of the head and knocked me unconscious.

M: NSP.

J: I see the bear rolling my body down the hill. I'm looking down. I'm going up in the sky.

M: Can you see a light to go toward?

J: Yes.

M: What do you find?

J: There are three people: my father, my mother, and my sister.

M: What happens?

J: We're all together in a big embrace. They're glad to see me.

M: Is your mother from that life anyone from this life?

J: No.

M: Did you have a good relationship with your mother in that life?

J: It seems to be alright.

M: Is there anything you'd like to tell your mother in that life?

J: I don't really know who she is.

M: Is there anything you want to tell your father from that life.

J: That I tried to be a dutiful son.

M: What does he say back?

J: You were a dutiful son.

M: What does your mother in that life say to you?

J: She says something like we're all proud of you.

M: Anything else?

J: She's glad I came home to them.

M: Now that she's said that to you, is there anything you'd like to say to her?

J: I guess I felt she abandoned us when she died.

M: What do you want to say to her about that now? Do you realize now that she couldn't help that?

J: Yes. She says something like she died to make us closer. We needed to work on things that we couldn't have worked on if she'd stayed in the picture.

M: What kind of things?

J: Taking care of each other.

M: *Why don't you ask her if you did okay with that?*

J: *She says I was a very good son.*

M: *Is there anything else?*

J: *She died when I was just a boy. I'm sorry I didn't get to spend more years with her.*

M: *You want to tell her that?*

J: *She says we have forever to be together.*

M: *Is there anything else you want to talk to your mother about?*

J: *No.*

M: *Is there anything you want to talk to your sister about?*

J: *Just that I loved her, and that it never mattered to me the way she was. It was kind of what I loved about her in a way.*

M: *When you gave yourself instruction to come into this life, you wanted to find the source of the anger you have toward your mother. Do you see some anger in your relationship with your sister in that life that you have to resolve?*

J: *No.*

M: *Was there any anger you might associate to your life or your death? Were you angry about dying?*

J: *No, I didn't mind dying. I wasn't particularly thrilled with the way I died, but I didn't mind dying.*

M: *I'm going to count to five and you will meet your Higher self or a beam of light to which you can direct any questions about the lessons of that lifetime. (1-2-3-4-5.) I want you to ask what is the message from that life that I need to bring back to this life?*

(The spirit of my father from this lifetime appears.)

J: My father says, "You see, the parts of her you thought were missing are still there, even if you don't see them now."

M: What parts is he referring to?

J: Her lovingness. Her attentiveness.

M: Ask him if there's any other message to bring back from that lifetime.

J: "You spend too much time on her. She is not your problem."

M: Ask what is your problem.

J: "You can't love yourself."

M: Ask him if he can help you to love yourself.

J: "I always wanted to teach you, but before I didn't know how."

M: So what does he know now that's important to you?

J: He says, "You must allow yourself to be guided by the spirit within you."

***

This session did a number of things for me. Mostly, it helped me to view my mother in a more benign light. Secondly, it made me realize that the source of my problems was internal, and that I had always had the power to heal what felt wrong inside. It broke the mounting frustration I felt regarding my mother's behavior, because it no longer seemed like my anger had anything to do with her. Consequently, I stopped feeling controlled by the obligation to please her, the guilt that resulted whenever I chose not to, and the disillusionment that arose when I tried and failed.

My enduring anger at her had always been my own projection onto her of the disappointment I felt in myself. In my own consuming sense of failure and incompetence, I had made her my judge. I could not see that all along it was *I* who could not overlook my shortcomings and imperfections.

Perhaps, I did learn to be hypercritical, demanding, rigid, and unappreciative of myself at my mother's knee, but in the final analysis, she is not the person who has mistreated me the most in my life. I am.

The rigid and demanding side of me finds it hard to tolerate the side of me which doesn't perform to its impossible standards. The creative, impulsive part of me despises the dictator part because it will not allow it the freedom it needs to express itself. The end result is a lot of abandoned ideas and projects, a long series of failed and troubled relationships, and a great deal of anger.

But resolution of a problem such as this goes beyond simple identification. It's been important for me to accept my mistakes, past and present. I now try to look at my mistakes not as setbacks, but as experiences which actually enhance the journey toward greater self-love and approval. I now try to relax the standards and forgive myself for messing up. It isn't always easy, but reversing a pattern of low self-esteem doesn't happen overnight.

Letting myself be guided by the spirit within me is something I'm only starting to understand and explore, and I deal more with this area in later chapters. It seems I've spent so much of my life giving over my power to people like my mother, I'm not always sure how to use that power once it's been reclaimed.

Lately, there have been some new styles of therapy which focus their attention on the needs of an *inner child*, and encourage us to become better parents to ourselves than our original ones were. While I like and applaud the spirit of this thinking in its helping people to grow up and start taking responsibility for themselves, I think it's hard for people to lose the mental image with which the inner child burdens them. For me, it has been a major breakthrough to envision my inner self as an evolved, higher and more powerful spirit, instead of the pained and damaged child I used to see there.

In the same vein, we should turn a similar eye on our parent and see them not just as *parent*, but as a fellow soul on the road of life, who actually has her own path to follow. Even after we grow up, it seems, we remain a little child when it comes to emotional issues with our parents, and our expectations of them may not always be appropriate. We still demand, the way we did as children, that their behavior be above reproach. But *every* soul we encounter in life is simply fulfilling its destiny. We must learn to respect the right of others to make their own choices, even if they are our parents, and their choices are poor ones. We must even respect the sole ownership that people have over their pain; it is not our responsibility to fix it, nor our right.

People can only do what feels right to them. We all follow the details of a hidden agenda to which no one else is privy. I cannot criticize the choices my mother made or failed to make in her life, because I don't know where she's been or what she set out to do here.

What surprised me most about the regression—and one of the reasons why I don't believe sessions like this are consciously created—was how untroubled my relationship with Greta was. I had expected going in, as had my therapist, that the relationship I uncovered would be fraught with tension and perhaps some tragic turn of events, for which I had never forgiven the person who is now my mother. Instead, I found the individual with whom I now had such trouble, to be completely endearing. I was happy to be in her company, and felt lost and alone without her. If I gave up anything for her—like the prospect of marriage—it didn't feel like a sacrifice. I was content and even felt privileged to be her protector.

I now believe that I chose my mother in this lifetime not so much for the purpose of settling a score between us, but out of love for her.   If someone reappears again and again throughout our history, it occurs not so much because of unresolved issues—as these can be resolved with other souls or different karmic work—but because the love between these two souls is so deep and compelling. In fact, I believe, that it is with those we love most that we choose to do our deepest karmic work, because those souls are the ones from whom we feel most likely to receive the one thing we ultimately return to earth to retrieve—forgiveness for our mistakes.

***

Five years have now passed since the above regression occurred. What I was able to initially garner from that session, I soon learned, was simply a foundation for what I would later come to know about my mother and me. Without the benefit of this past-life recall, I honestly don't know how I might have dealt with the experiences which were to come our way.

It actually took many years for us to realize that our mother's strange habits, personality changes and socially inappropriate behaviors had a physiological basis to them, and were not due to just some kind of old age orneriness, which many believed them to be. Shortly before my mother died this past April, after so many tests, and doctors' examinations and discussions and time, not to mention the many more sad chapters in my mother's life, we finally received a diagnosis with which we and her various doctors and specialists seemed content, a disorder known as OPC, which stands for *olivopontocerebellar degeneration*, an incurable and eventually fatal neurological disease.

The effects of this disease are numerous, insidious and heartbreaking. OPC affects behavior, appetite, sleep habits, judgment, memory, mood, balance, motor control, speech, awareness and personality, and it systematically transformed my mother into someone completely different from the woman she had been. Strangely enough, my mother became as time went on, more and more like Greta, and as my father said, although I did not realize the prescience of his remark, "the parts of her (I) thought were missing, (were) still there."

The most striking change for me in my mother's personality was how affectionate she became. In fact, in her final days, as she became quite childlike, she would freely approach, embrace and even kiss perfect strangers. It seemed to me that what the layers of rigid socialization revealed as they were peeled away by her increasing disorientation, was a woman who had been virtually starved for affection.

When I sat in the car with her now, she would no longer babble on about her problems. Oftentimes she would sit and gaze lovingly at me, spontaneously grab my hand and kiss it, tell me I was beautiful—as if this had nothing whatsoever to do with her—and that she loved me, always that she loved me. Well, here she is, I thought with irony to myself, looking across the seat at a woman whose unremitting disappointment with life had finally taken away her sanity; here's the loving, attentive mother I once mistrusted the existence of, the person I so desperately wanted evidence of that perhaps out of some elaborate gesture of love and self-sacrifice she had actually endeavored to give her to me. (Be careful what you wish for, they say, you might just get it.)

What anger I hadn't been able to eradicate completely from my feelings for my mother prior to the blossoming of her illness, OPC forced me to unload. With my mother I was obliged to travel to a place where expectation and disappointment and indignation had no relevance—a place of unabiding compassion. With terrible eloquence, my mother's illness made certain before she ever let go of her foothold on this earth that no trace of resentment or disapproval or even aggravation would endure in me. It made its show upon my mother so macabre and ironic and incredible that the lessons it had to teach me about love and sorrow could never be ignored or misunderstood or forgotten.

In the last two years of my mother's life, when he became too concerned for her safety to allow her to continue to stay on her own, my brother Bracken moved my mother to a care facility for the elderly. I would visit from Connecticut on occasion; he would fill me in on the changes that had taken place since our last talk, and the two of us would never fail to sit and shake our heads in wonder at the person she had become. Who would have ever thought, we would say to each other, in a hundred million years, who would have ever thought?

It was staggering, oftentimes frightening to see these changes in her. Physically, OPC has an impact on the body which is similar to Parkinson's disease. By the end, my mother's hands and jaw shook constantly, her legs took on a shuffled gait. Her whole frame just seemed to shrink and hollow out, but most startling was the change in that once beautiful face, which after so many years of unrelenting sorrow became frozen into a tragic, wide-eyed howl.

The changes in me, however, and in my relationship with my mother, were miraculous. The sicker and more helpless my mother became, the harder it became for me to continue to hold back love from her. I didn't feel ashamed of her anymore, because now I knew who she was. I didn't struggle so much to please her, because I knew now what she wanted. "I love you," I would say to her now, hugging her as we parted, "I love you no matter what."

Sometimes I look back on my mother's life as I now believe we should each wisely reflect on our own parents' lives. I try and step out of the action, and view it in whole as a sort of allegory, if you will. What did my mother's life and her illusions teach me about my own life?

It is only natural that we are like our parents in our habits and tastes, behavior and limitations. They are the schools at which we learn our first lessons, at which we shape our values, our expectations and our opinions of ourselves. As children, we become as accurate a mimicry of our parents as we can—we do it for approval, mostly, but also because we don't know there are options. As adults, I believe there comes a point when the mirror gets turned around; we begin to take a jaundiced view of the role models from whence we sprang. We begin to ask: what's wrong with this picture?

But the ensuing realizations about where our parent falls short is less a breakthrough than it is a heartbreak. They're not perfect, we discover, and we turn away from them in shame and disgust. We expect them perhaps to justify themselves to us—as I did, when I wrote my letter of anger to my mother—and they are mystified because to them, nothing has changed. They *always* knew they were imperfect.

If we have any obligation to our parents at all, it is probably to accept from them with love and gratitude—and no judgment—what they had the generosity to show us in their beautiful imperfect way *doesn't* work. My mother showed me many things through the story that was her life: don't just look at the empty half of the glass, don't keep joy at bay, don't expect perfection, don't become your own tyrant, and never ever be so foolish as to hold back love, because it will break down any barrier you put against it with a force that is sure and catastrophic.

My mother left this earth quietly one Sunday evening in April, 1994. In a matter of days, I picked up the presence of her, as I had always been able to do with my father. She began to leave messages in my head, and still frequently does, in the form of song lyrics—what else?—which are always very loving and not infrequently clever and humorous, as well.

The way I recognize my mother now is by her demeanor; I can only describe her as a being of unrelenting joy, a joy that borders on a light giddiness, with equal contagion to the dark, dark angel she once was. You see, I got my wish there, as well. It seems my mother finally met and became that woman I saw her capture so briefly one summer evening in her sister's kitchen. That woman's smile beams through my mind each time I think of my mother now, and often I will hear her clear beautiful voice—as I heard it all my life—ringing across the heavens.

"Acceptance"

Chapter Three

Acceptance

So much of what happens in life is prophetic. So much of what comes our way, we realize, in hindsight, we saw coming; we had an inkling of or a gut feeling about. Does it prepare us better for what comes? If we had recognized the clues, we ask ourselves, how would it have changed anything?

I think it comes down to an issue of acceptance, really, when these prophetic moments occur. What it says to us in hindsight is no, you could not have changed this even though you knew. This event was planned well in advance. This event was meant to be. Everything led to this, and everything now leads away.

I dreamed of and *anticipated* my father's death, a close friend's breast cancer, and the premature birth of my son. But I have come to learn that these insights into the future are not warnings, they are part of the process of the event, a simple blip on the continuum of time, which the soul—over whom time has no dominion—has borne witness to even before it occurred in thought.

If I were to be honest, I would have to say I knew of my brother's death at least two years before it occurred. I saw it in his face that summer, and dismissed it from my conscious mind because it wasn't something I desired to have registered there. Earlier that year in fact, I had become deeply depressed and strangely haunted by some childhood memories of him. I remember sitting in my therapist's office recounting the day Don had come home from the service on leave.

I was seven years old when I walked in from school that day and to my surprise found a soldier's hat flung across the living room sofa. When my mother explained that Don was out visiting his friends, I eagerly went outside to the top of a hill behind our house and waited for him to return home. After what seemed like hours, the family car finally pulled up, and I took off running to him, so fast down the hill I wasn't sure I could stop.

Just as I reached him, he scooped me up high into the air, like some wobbly little plane settling into its course. I was relieved to meet the same person who had left me months before, somehow assured that he would always remain safe and intact, now that I could lean my face against him and circle my arms around his neck.

It was just a simple story about a skinny little girl getting a hug from a big brother in uniform, too simple to convey the complexity of feeling underneath or the tears that rolled relentlessly down my cheeks as I reminisced. Inside I felt such grief, a piercing sense of sadness that no amount of tears could relax.

My therapist, on observing this, asked why I thought the memory affected me so much, and I said it had to do with the sense that everything had been completely perfect to me in that moment. Growing up, I'd discovered that life didn't serve up many moments like that, and all I was doing now was assigning this one its true value. Why I felt compelled to do that, however, after so many years, remained a mystery to me.

My therapist suggested that it was memory of the leaving rather than his homecoming that filled me with such sadness. She felt that my unfortunate placement in my family—youngest of six children—had forced me to witness at an impressionable period of my life, the gradual disintegration of my family unit. This buried grief had been focussed on Don because as my eldest brother, he had been the first to go, and his leaving home had heralded for me the imminent departure of my other siblings.

Looking back now, five years after his death, I realize the reason for these feelings was not so complex. The point of all the sadness about Don turned out to be no more than precognition—some small, undetected window into the future that quietly opened itself in my head. What was buried underneath the swell of emotion I couldn't comprehend was the foresight that one day soon my brother would once again be leaving, and this time he *wouldn't* come back.

***

My brother was diagnosed with what is known as glioblastoma, a form of malignant brain tumor. A post-operative evaluation by his doctors revealed that the tumor was in such advanced stages, there was nothing they could do to reverse or cure it. Don died in his home, exactly one month later, at the age of 47.

That summer, the summer of 1989, my brothers and sisters and I spent the month of July and the early part of August shuttling back and forth between our own lives and the very new and weird reality of our brother's dying. Adrift as we seemed in this sad mission, our past with Don became central and all-important to us. It was the only reality we knew after all, not this one of him so fragile and inaccessible. Confronted with his death, we held fast to the moments we shared with him thirty and forty years previous, moments we had once let go of voluntarily when they didn't matter quite so much.

When I was home in Connecticut, I tried to remain energized and involved, and yet, ready to slip out and return at a moment's notice to Kansas and the sagging hold my brother now had on his life there. I couldn't really feel part of either place, however, and the action seemed to carry on in spite of me, like two movies being shown in different sections of the same theater. Sometimes I sat and watched one, sometimes the other, feeling I'd lost track of the plot line in both.

It was the first acknowledgement of grief—the shock—that fuzzy, insulated sensation that made me question whether this experience could really be mine. Perhaps I had gone to sleep, and awakened into someone else's not-so-pleasant life. Surely, tomorrow morning I would get it right and not sleep through my stop.

This phase, however, was punctuated by occasional reminders that this *was* my tragedy after all, and life as I knew it was now being permanently altered in some deranged, haphazard way. The reminders would arrive unexpectedly in a feeling that spilled through my body like the cold, tingly wash of some sickening drug, and each time it happened, it seemed I heard the news of my brother's impending death for the first time.

Everyone who has experienced a death in the family knows the common stages of the mourning process, the shock and denial, the anger and abandonment. Some are fortunate enough to reach beyond these stages to embrace acceptance and even reconciliation, but whatever the individual process, grief is a common course that everyone must travel over at some point or other in life.

There is another aspect of grief, though, that cannot be shared. From the moment I first learned of my brother's illness, I felt vulnerable and disoriented. I was holding my finger in a dyke of emotions that threatened to unload if the least disappointment or stress added its own weight to the overflow. I expected others to understand the precariousness of my state, to deal with me from a respectful distance, and suspend any expectations they might normally have of me. Surely my husband and son could help fill the strange, cold hole blown through my heart. Surely the plain fact that my brother was dying warranted me protection, indulgence and slack.

But my brother's dying was *not* a plain fact. It was not ordinary or simple or in some ways communicable. There was a part of it—the deepest part—which *had* no common denominator. You see, I wanted to say to the world at large, only Don realizes that I am the little girl who stood watching him from the front lawn while he played ball in the street. No one but me understands why he bought me a red sweater for Christmas two years in a row. There is no other person here, I longed to explain, who can feel the significance of these things, no one but the individual who is tied to me because of them—and he is now forever unavailable for comment.

***

Philosophically, I never had much trouble accepting the loss of my brother. I had experienced other grief, when my father died 10 years before, and I *knew* things about dying. I knew that the sadness would end, that the weight of it would lift, almost imperceptibly, and life would go on. I knew that after awhile the impulse to pick up the phone and call him would disappear; the longing to exchange opinions with him about current events or family matters would go away. After awhile the change that took place in my world the day my brother departed from it, would no longer be a change. Someday my brother's absence from my life would be *status quo*.

These are the things I knew, even early on. But this understanding didn't prepare me for the odd disquiet which now took up residence somewhere inside. I was troubled by something I can only describe as silence—because there is no other common word for it—between my brother and me. I hadn't felt this with my father. In fact I had always been aware, uncomfortably at first, of an ethereal *presence* of him. Sometimes he would even seem to pass through my room, early in the morning as I woke before dawn, leaving messages, not with individual words, but in whole chunks of thought that would suddenly be transplanted into my head. I stopped feeling the absence of my father when I finally realized I wasn't imagining the strange proximity I actually had to him.

But with Don, there was nothing, just something that felt like empty, black space. Sometimes I would try and talk into the space, but I never felt anything come back from the other end.

It was six months after my brother's death that I began past-life regression therapy. I was showing all the classic signs of mourning—the despondency and detachment, the oversleeping and under-eating, the impatience and anger—but I never recognized them as symptoms of grief until it was suggested by Marion. I resisted her conclusions—as I had often done with myself—that I hadn't actually accepted this death, and that there was something more deep-seated in my emotions concerning my brother's absence.

But death, like any other experience, can be overlaid with emotional debris from the past. As it turned out, my brother has preceded me in death at least twice before, and both of these experiences were significantly more dramatic in circumstance for the person I was to him then. In both instances—once when he was my older brother in 5th century Morocco and again as my father in 19th century France—my life was altered irreparably after he died. Here, in this life, his death triggered the emotional pain from these prior lives, and while part of me reasoned that life would go on, a deeper part of me affirmed that nothing would ever be the same, that life was a pointless process that had to be endured until I could be with him again. It now appeared that the empty, silent space, which separated my brother Don and me, was the rest of my life.

***

The transcript which follows is taken from my past-life recall of a life I shared with my brother in Morocco. It is the regression which unfolded when I asked what significant lives we had spent together and how remembering them could resolve my current grief:

J: I get the word camel-driver. I don't know what that means.

M: Are you the camel-driver?

J: No, I think he is.

M: What is his name?

J: Something like Caleb or Caliph.

M: Are you there too?

J: Yes.

M: Are you male or female?

J: I'm not sure.

M: I'll count to three and you'll be sure. 1-2-3.

J: Male.

M: Can you tell me your name?

J: Simon.

M: How old are you?

J: 14.

M: How old is Caleb?

J: 18.

M: Are you related to each other?

J: We're brothers.

M: What are you wearing?

J: I have on a long robe. Sandals and some type of headdress.

M: What country are you in?

J: Morocco.[1]

M: What year is it?

J: 429 (A.D.)

M: What are the two of you doing?

J: We're waiting for battle.

M: What kind of battle? Who are you going to fight?

J: Some tribes that are coming down from Spain.[2]

---

[1]   From about 40 A.D., Morocco was occupied by a tribe of people known as the Berbers, who had Hamito-Semitic roots.
[2]   Morocco was briefly invaded by the Vandals, from 429-430 A.D.

M: Are you going to fight, too?

J: Yes, I think so.

M: Tell me what's happening.

J: We're in a desert area. We're either on horses or camels or both. (1-2-3.) I'm on a camel. My brother's on a horse.

M: Go to the next significant part. (Hereafter NSP.)

J: We're in a battle. It's really very chaotic.

M: What are you fighting with?

J: Swords.

M: Can you describe them?

J: Big and thick. I don't have one.

M: Tell me what's happening.

J: It's very hard to tell what's going on. All I see is a lot of rushing around and things sort of clashing together.

M: Is it the men on the animals clashing together when they're fighting each other? Is that it?

J: I'm trying to figure out if I'm in the battle or just watching it. I seem real close to it, but not participating. And I don't feel my life is threatened.

M: Did they perhaps give you something to drink before the battle to make you feel that way?

J: No, I don't think so.

M: NSP.

J: There are some things that are burning and a lot of smoke.

M: Could you describe it?

J: I'm pretty far away from the fire. It's on the other side of the field. Someone had a torch and it's lying there burning. My brother and I are walking around the bodies.

M: NSP.

J: There's some kind of palace or mosque or something. We're outside on a walkway near a fountain.

M: Is the battle over?

J: Yes.

M: Are you and your brother both okay?

J: I think so.

M: What's happening here by this fountain?

J: We're talking to some women. He's interested in this one woman, and she's interested in him. He goes off with her.

M: NSP.

J: I think it's a wedding.

M: Who's getting married?

J: My brother and this woman.

M: What's her name?

J: Something like Falia.

M: NSP.

J: There's some kind of headpiece that's cylindrical-shaped and very ornate. It's being placed on Falia's head, but I don't understand the significance.

M: Is it part of the marriage ceremony?

J: Yes. There's also a white lace canopy with gold posts over their heads. It's covered with white flowers.

M: NSP.

J: I believe that I've discovered that Falia is unfaithful to my brother.

M: How long have they been married?

J: Two years.

M: NSP.

J: I see some really high thing. I'm standing on it. I'm not sure what it is. It's really high, like a platform or something. It's some device that's used to kill people.

M: Is the device on the platform with you?

J: I'm standing on the device itself, but I don't know what I'm doing there. There doesn't seem to be anyone around.

M: Can you describe it? What does it look like?

J: It's very tall and then has a cross piece with something hanging from the cross piece like a blade. I'm up on the cross-piece; I'm fixing it or something. It's like a version of the guillotine. It's designed to kill people. I'm on the cross piece where the rope is attached. I'm fixing it.[3]

M: NSP.

J: This girl is being executed.

M: Your brother's wife?

---

[3] As I understood it, the execution device had to be set by a member of the dishonored family.

J: Yes. There's a lot of people standing around. She has on a white dress and her hands are tied behind her back.

M: Is she being executed because she was unfaithful to her husband?

J: Yes.

M: How does he feel about this?

J: He's very upset about it. He doesn't have a lot of choice. It's become public knowledge, and once that happens, it's out of his hands. That's the way the law works.

M: NSP.

J: My brother and I are in a room talking. He's crying because he misses his wife. He can't let anyone know he feels this way, because he is supposed to believe in the law, and that it was right for her to be killed. He's not supposed to mourn her.

M: NSP.

J: I'm sitting on a rock. It's very steep. I'm worrying about my brother. He's very disgraced and shamed; he doesn't want to go out anymore. I'm worried that if people find out how he feels, he will be more shamed. Everyone will shun him; he won't be viewed as a true man, because he's mourning this woman who betrayed him.

M: NSP.

J: My brother has committed suicide. I think he slit his throat. He's in his bed, and there's a lot of blood all over the sheets.

M: NSP.

J: It's a funeral for my brother.

M: NSP.

J: I'm outside in that same area where my brother met Falia. I'm walking by myself and feeling as if I would like to just get away from this life. I want to go to a monastery.

M: NSP.

J: I think that's what I did. The monastery is made out of stucco-like material. I feel very good there, very peaceful.

M: Can you tell me the name of the monastery?

J: Anastasius.

M: Does that have some meaning in your language?

J: I don't know.

M: 1-2-3.

J: I get the word gold. Black gold. Something about some lamps that might be the type that burn incense, but I think they burn oil. It's a scented oil.

M: What else do you see? What do you wear there?

J: A robe with a tie, and some sandals that appear to be made of rope.

M: Do they still call you the same name there?

J: I think they call me Peter.

M: Is it a Christian monastery?[4]

J: Yes.

M: Are you still in Morocco?

J: Yes.

---

[4] Monasticism started in Egypt between 250 and 355 A.D., and spread throughout the Byzantine Empire, of which Morocco had been a part since the late 300's. However, it had actually been Christianized under Roman rule much earlier.

M: *You said you feel very peaceful there. Can you describe what you do during the day?*

J: *I work in the flower gardens.*

M: *NSP.*

J: *I'm in a room there. I'm getting a bit bored with things.*

M: *How long have you been there.*

J: *Three years.*

M: *How old are you now?*

J: *23.*

M: *What do you decide to do?*

J: *I want to leave.*

M: *Are you able to do that?*

J: *I gave them all my money when I came here. I don't really have anything to go back to, and that's what stops me.*

M: *NSP.*

J: *I've left and I've become a camel-driver.*

M: *NSP.*

J: *I'm in a sandstorm, and one of the men I'm with has been wounded in some way, thrown from a camel. I think he's been trampled by a camel. He's lying on his side, howling.*

M: *NSP.*

J: *I'm an old man. I'm still living in the desert. I'm sitting inside a tent, looking out at the sky. It's very blue.*

M: *I want you to go to the moment of your death.*

J: I'm in a tent. I'm just dying of old age. I'm very tired.

M: How old are you?

J: 83.

M: Is anyone with you?

J: No.

M: Does anyone take care of you?

J: No, I'm like a hermit.

M: Go to the moment of your death.

J: I'm going up into the sky. The sky is very, very blue.

M: NSP.

J: I see a lot of spirals of light and a swirl of light that goes up and down, almost like a roller coaster.

M: Do you see anyone that you talk to?

J: My brother's there.

M: What does he do?

J: He embraces me.

M: Does he say anything?

J: He understands how much I've missed him.

M: Is there anything you want to say to your brother about that life?

J: I hope I don't have to wait that long to see him again.

M: I'll count to five and you will see your Higher self, which will enable you to ask questions about that life. 1-2-3-4-5. Ask your Higher self what was the meaning of that life; what are you to bring from that life into this life?

J: Patience.

M: Is there any other message that's important?

J: There's nothing wrong with the devotion I feel for my brother.

M: Is there any other message that your Higher self wants to give to you at this time?

J: That it's okay to mourn my brother, but I shouldn't give over my whole life to it.

M: Any other message?

J: No.

M: Does your brother have any other message for you before you leave?

J: He misses me, too.

M: Is there any other message you want to give him before you leave?

J: No.

M: Can you look back and forgive everyone in that life who did you any wrong?

J: Yes.

M: Can you forgive yourself for any wrongdoing?

J: Yes.

M: I want you to leave all of the sadness and hurt of that life in that life and just bring back with you all of the strength of the patience and love that you experienced in that life.

The after effects of this regression were quite profound for me. At first, I couldn't shake the terrible longing I had felt as this loyal younger brother, who turned over his whole life to mourning. It was as if the real grieving for Don, which I had held back until then, now swept over my life with a force which was too powerful to check. During the days immediately after the session, I wondered what the point of it had been. I felt worse, really. For one thing it had been extremely painful to leave my brother's presence again at the end of the regression; it had felt so soothing to hold him.

But the feelings turned out to be only aftershock. It was the heaviness of all that old grief finally taking its leave from my heart. After a week or so, the weight of it lifted, and it has never returned. I realized my attempts to deny myself proper mourning for my brother had been initiated out of the fear that the grieving would take over my life, and transform it into nothing more than a long and arduous wait for my own death.

***

As time passes away now from my brother's dramatic exit from this life, I have attempted to understand the process which led him to conclude that death was his best option, just as I suppose Simon once examined Caleb's similarly drawn conclusion. When I looked at Don, I only ever saw this man who charmed everyone who met him. He was bright and witty and perceptive. I enjoyed talking to him more than just about anybody else I can think of, because he always saw things other people overlooked and remembered things everyone else had long forgotten. It's what made him such a great storyteller; it's what gave him such wide appeal with others, his family, friends, children, neighbors and colleagues. Maybe it's the kind of thing people always say about someone who dies, that everyone liked him, but with Don it was really true—everyone did.

In 1981, about eight years before his death, my brother was diagnosed with the crippling disease known as multiple sclerosis. Though he never completely lost his ability to walk because of it, his motor responses deteriorated rapidly at the end of his life, due to the effects of a completely unrelated tumor which insinuated itself under the bone of his skull like a large, menacing hand. The MS was the reason why various neurological symptoms stemming purely from the tumor went unchecked until it was far too late to do anything. Don's worst fear, that he would end up an invalid from his MS, proved to be unfounded. But the fear itself provided something with far more malevolent power, something that would end the life which had become so limited he no longer wished to live it.

I always said that Don's MS was not the thing which concerned me, it was his complete inability to accept himself as a person who had it. He used to say that my mother looked at him as if he were "damaged goods," and I'm sure I know the look to which he referred. The unfortunate part was that he saw himself that way, too. He was ashamed of his dependency on others to give him a hand now and then. He was ashamed of the awkwardness and embarrassment he sometimes saw on their faces whenever that happened.

Multiple sclerosis moved Don's life to a place he found unlivable, despite the fact that it always remained—and for that matter still remains—rich with people who loved him. What I believe he saw to be the thing that prevented him from remaining the agent of his own life, was in actuality the same thing which was created to teach him otherwise.

I don't believe our lives are limited by anything unless we ourselves define it as a limitation. The reality is that we live in a universe which is limitless in what it provides us. All we need to do is accept what it offers us.

Two years before my brother died, he was driving to a business conference a few hours from his home in Kansas, when a blizzard blew up unexpectedly. At some point during the tedious journey in the snow, he realized he had a flat tire, and pulled the car off the interstate onto a cloverleaf. Due to the advanced stages of his MS, Don had difficulty balancing himself, and changing the tire proved an impossible task. He tried several times to manage it, but finally gave up and got in the car to wait.

After a short while, an old, battered car pulled in front of his, and out stepped an elderly black man who began to change the flat tire. After he had finished, Don called to him to come and sit for a moment so they could talk. The man revealed that he was a minister from a church on the other side of the state. Don was surprised to hear this and asked what was he doing so far away, and the man replied quite simply: "God sent me here today to help you."

It's difficult for me to imagine how Don might have responded to the man after he said that. Apparently, he offered him a contribution to his church, which the minister refused. What I am sure of, though, is that my brother, even after having witnessed this individual's miraculous intervention in his life, never believed for a second that the old man—whom I now believe was in all likelihood, an angel—had been sent by God.

This was not the only time that opportunities of help and guidance came my brother's way after he developed MS. There was a man I found out about through a minister of my church in New York City, who also had MS, and ran an ongoing series of inspirational talks for people who needed to learn to cope with the disease. Coincidentally, the man worked out of Kansas City, and when I called my brother with his name, he had not only heard of him, but had attended one of his talks. To my knowledge, he never attended any more.

There was a woman my brother Tom learned about, whom he wanted Don to contact. Apparently, this woman had been told by neurologists that her MS would put her in a wheel chair in five years time. Six years later, after developing her own special program of physical therapy, she passed by these same doctors' offices as she completed the last leg of a marathon in which she was running.

We inundated my brother with books on self-healing, positive thinking, and special diets for MS sufferers. He did make some attempt at vitamin therapy and changing his diet. He worked with a stationary bike to keep his legs toned, and tried acupuncture for a while. And I'm sure he read all of the books we sent him. But, what it always came down to was a lack of faith in his own ability to cure himself, in his own ability to survive against the odds. He had admiration and respect for those who could, for those in touch with their spiritual side, but when we talked about the possibility of that happening to him, he would simply say: "That isn't me; it's not for me."

During the last weeks of my brother's life, my sister Nancy went to Don's office to make some copies of the medical claims we were helping my sister-in-law process. On top of my brother's desk was a plaque on a stand, inscribed with the words of Winston Churchill: "Never, NEVER give in!" My sister felt this plaque should be rescued from his office and placed beside my brother's bed where he could see it. As she reached over to take it, she noticed a little piece of paper taped to the front rim of Don's desk. The paper read: "Who will stop the rain?"

While Don could admire, perhaps more passionately than most, the power within others to meet head-on whatever misfortune came their way, he could somehow never locate that same power within himself. Viewing himself as he did—a man who was flawed and undeserving of victory—it perhaps never occurred to him that the only person who could stop the rain was the one who was asking himself that question.

***

After my brother died, it took many years before I was able to break the *silence* between us and detect for the first time some sense of his spirit around me. I had accomplished this with no real effort when it came to my deceased parents. But Don's absence seemed enduring; it would at times perplex me, and at other times wound me. I worried about his well-being, though I knew in my heart he was at peace, and fretting about such things was needless. And I certainly missed him, I have to say. With my clairaudience skills all nicely honed from years of listening to my dead father, I was more than ready to talk, so where was he?

Though I guess I was able to come to terms with the *fact* of my brother's death soon after the regression, I don't believe I accepted—until quite recently—that this outcome was the best alternative for him. Frankly, I looked at his death as a cop-out and a failure. While I accused him of lacking faith and trust in the process of his life, I misjudged the wisdom of his soul to know the proper course for him to take. And it was wrong of me to have done so.

My experiences with past-life regression taught me *intellectually* that death is not a failure in life, but a different, even higher form of it. Nothing, it told me, is ended by death; nothing is lost. It is simply the soul making another passage, taking another turn in the road of its eternal process.

Emotionally, however, I could not accept this truth about my brother's death. "Why couldn't you have hung on?" I would say to him from time to time. Little wonder he never bothered to respond.

I despaired over my brother's decision to leave us. I mistakenly believed that he had left too soon—in the middle of the test—he had gone without first making the grade. I was angry with him for not playing the game as I might have done had I been dealt his hand; I was annoyed that he had failed to choose the other options we had all laid out for him.

Why do we harbor such regret? Why do we forever question the life process of our fellow human beings? It is, I think, a sort of two-fold lack of faith: first of all, there is the doubt that *the life we are living will continue unimpeded, regardless of the departure of another*. We all have our own journeys to make, and while another soul may be making *his* journey alongside ours, it is not possible or even desirable that he move in the same direction.

The second doubt is that *there is meaning and purpose and design to each and everything that occurs*, that there is no such thing as a mistake, whether it be in our own life or in the life of another. And this is true whether we choose to see it that way or not. The perfection of life, after all, is a constant; it is not limited by whether or not we can accept it.

Several months ago, while I was out driving my car, thinking about my brother and wondering as I often have since his death what it was that kept him so distant, I suddenly felt a sensation like butterflies in my stomach. Then the strangest thing occurred. I got this very strong image of him sitting in the passenger seat beside me, snickering the way he used to when he thought he was pulling something over on me. He had his hands tucked under his legs and he was leaning forward in a spasm of laughter. I shook my head and smiled in acknowledgement, realizing that the barrier between us had finally been broken, and that all along it was I—by refusing to accept his death—who had avoided an important test.

Since then, I have apologized to my brother for viewing his decision to leave life here as a flawed and premature one, and I thank him for the insights his silence brought me. Recently I asked him if *he* ever saw his death as a failure. "No," he answered firmly, "if anything, it was an advancement."

***

Once in a while, I think back to the day my brother came home from the service and I ran down the hill into his arms. It's a sweet memory, and the sadness it used to bring me is no longer present. There's still a kind of pull sometimes in my heart and stomach, when I think of him that spring day long ago, but it's more like the leap of anticipation than it is regret.

I have come to understand that at some point, somewhere within each of us, we hold foresight into the moment our own existence in this world will come to an end—our own homecoming. For me, I imagine there will be the same long, bright tunnel through which we are all said to float away from the earth, but at the end of mine, I envision a particular hill with a long, grassy slope, and down that hill I see my brother Don, running fast.

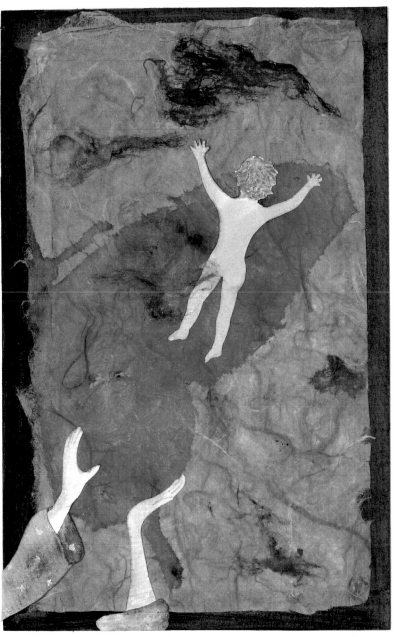

"Letting Go"

Chapter Four

Letting Go

The first time I saw Ryan's face was three days before he was born. That night in a dream, I found myself driving in a car with a boy of about seven, who appeared to be my son. We were going to meet my father, who, though dead, had agreed to come and see us. The boy and I were both anxious for my father to like him. I parked the car on a street I remember from childhood, and got out to wait. Soon my father's car pulled up across the street, and he came over to us. He got into the back seat of my car along with the boy, and they began to talk.

It seemed they were discussing sports, which my father loved in his lifetime, and which my son now loves in his. In the dream, my son made some observation about a particular game or player, and my father brightened and acknowledged the insight as a good one.

In that moment, my son looked up at me for the first time, and gave me an odd and knowing smile. The smile said he was relieved to know his grandfather liked him; it said he could see that I, too, was pleased. It said he understood what I was thinking, and that it wouldn't ever take more than this brief and particular look for us to say everything which needed to be said to one another.

The boy's smile and the brightness of his sweet face, turned up towards me, stayed clear and precise in my memory. When Ryan was born soon after, five weeks short of full term, I understood him to be the boy in the dream; I think I would have recognized him anywhere.

I was surprised to have a son, actually. I had always seen myself as a mother of daughters, and the instinct I had while pregnant with him was that he would be a girl. For that reason the dream seemed peculiar, and yet, I could not ignore the strange, magnetic quality of the small face or the shy, funny smile which graced it.

That wasn't the last time I ever saw that smile. In what are always the simplest of moments, it will appear again on my son's face, magical and unexpected, like a rainbow. In those seconds of silent exchange between the two of us, I seem to recognize that part of the magic locked up in his expression is nothing more than familiarity, nothing more than the realization that that little face has been in my dreams for centuries.

***

In the first several months of my son's life, I was firmly convinced he would die and leave me. It had never been like me to have those kind of thoughts about anyone, but then, it had never been like me to feel so vulnerable to love before. This new vulnerability left me uncomfortable and worried. What would I do, I thought to myself, if something took him away from me? How would I go on with my life?

Ryan entered the world with a number of physical complications, a strange series of congenital anomalies for which no medical professional has ever been able to give us reasonable explanation. Fortunately, none of the defects were serious or life-threatening. Still, they involved three operations: abdominal surgery at five weeks to repair a small hole in his navel, a cranial operation at fourteen months to remove a bean-sized dermoid cyst from inside the front part of his skull, and later surgery to remove part of the same cyst that was growing inside the bridge of his nose, this two months before his second birthday. In addition, there was a heart murmur, a missing pulmonary artery, and a non-functional, partially-formed right lung. There was a funny noise when he exhaled, owing to a smaller than normal opening to the windpipe, and due to the space left by the tiny right lung, his heart was swung over into the center of his chest.

Ultimately, he was never anything but fine. He sailed through all his operations, and recuperated in half the expected time. He ate well, though they suspected he might not. He never developed pneumonia or the sumptuous lung they warned me he was prone to. The murmur receded and turned out to be nothing threatening to the stability of his heart. The noisy exhalation slowly faded, and the tiny, dark pink boy, who came into the world gasping for air, grew up tall and handsome and rosy-cheeked.

For me, the nightmarish quality of this particular period in my son's life and my own faded less quickly, even though I found that the wonder of his placid face throughout the wearisome rigors of hospitals and tests and specialists was the only sane point of reference I had ever been given. He was never a fretful or lethargic baby, but surprisingly alert and animated, engaging and even happy. His patience and good humor throughout the medical tedium that filled the first two years of his life was nothing short of astounding. Despite the less than ideal circumstances, he really seemed to enjoy it here. Life for Ryan was a groove.

I should have been able to focus on my son's overwhelming instinct for survival. I should have been able to focus on how well and happy he looked. I should have never let myself forget the calm, unassuming face that peered back at me through the glass of the incubator that first morning I saw him alive. But for a long time after the evidence showed that Ryan was a child who would flourish in the world—no matter what—I held back my enthusiasm. It somehow felt more warranted to hang onto the tired, anxious and angry mother I had become. Nothing and no one was going to catch me off guard, I thought; I was going to be prepared and ready and fully aware of any trouble that lay in wait for him.

I told myself it was the unpredictable nature of life I didn't trust, but in reality it was my own inadequacies as a mother which I believed to be the weak link in the security of my son's continued existence. Secretly, I feared there would be some moment of carelessness on my part, some indulgence in my own preoccupations, and Ryan would perish as a consequence. His dismissal from my life would be the only reasonable punishment for my irresponsible behavior.

All the medical rigmarole which, out of necessity, consumed a good deal of those initial years, in many ways reinforced my suspicions about my deficiencies as a mother. Hours after Ryan was born, he was moved by ambulance to a larger hospital, where he could receive the special medical care of a neonatal unit, with which his birth hospital wasn't equipped. Underneath the weird emotional confusion of my post-natal period was the understanding that this removal had been both curative and preventative, curative to remedy the damage I'd already done to him prenatally, and preventative in order to avoid any further mishandling.

Ryan stayed in the special care unit for three weeks, during which time I visited daily, tense and self-conscious, as if my inadequacies would be found out one day and I would be politely asked by the staff not to return. I felt I had no right to him. There was no feeling of familiarity when I held him, no true comprehension of what was happening to him physically, and certainly no continuity. Some days I would arrive at the hospital to find his previously inhabited cot or incubator either vacant or housing some other preemie, whose strange match-stick arms would flap back at me as I peered inside in search of my baby son. The nurses always seemed nonplussed by my indignation and panic in these moments, having, I suppose, never been in that situation themselves. "Where's my son? Where's my son?" I would shout at them, a question which at that point in my life was loaded with more emotion than I knew what to do with.

***

Long after Ryan's second birthday and the last of his hospitalizations, I still was given to occasional nightmares about losing him. One involved a trip on the London underground, in which I stepped momentarily out of the train, as it arrived at a stop, in order to determine if we had reached our departure point. Suddenly, the doors closed behind me, and the train sped off down the track with Ryan still aboard. The remainder of the dream was one of those common anxiety scenarios where I kept trying to get to him, and with each new turn of events only ended up further away from my destination. I woke up upset, and for days afterward the impact of those doors closing between us remained graphically reenacted in my mind.

I had just begun my past-life therapy with Marion, a month or two before, and at her suggestion, had been recording my dreams. We would work from time to on whatever dream material I felt significant, and this one seemed to be pressing me for exploration.

What was offered up by my unconscious to provide clarification for this dream was the lifetime just prior to my current one. The following account is the compilation of two regressions under the guidance of my therapist, and two which occurred during meditation on my own, an accessing skill which I acquired towards the end of my work with Marion.

During the second World War, I lived in Germany as a girl named Elsa, and was in my late teens at the time of my death in 1945. Ryan was my younger brother, by about ten years. My mother was a very stylish woman, and somewhat of a socialite. She and my father were political conservatives or Nationalists, a group which had lost power in Germany by 1938. When members of this once powerful group were overthrown by the Nazis, many joined the opposition. My parents apparently assumed our lives to be in jeopardy because of their political views and so they took my brother and me from our home in Berlin to the farm of a relative—a great aunt, I believe—in order to keep us from danger. We never heard from them after we were left on the farm, and it was assumed they had been captured and killed by the Nazis.

Somewhere towards the latter stages of the war, as the threat of invasion into Germany became imminent, the Nazis began to overtake farmhouses and land near the borders. The farm where we stayed was one of these, and my little brother and I were forced to move in with a nearby family.

It seems that by this time the elderly caretaker with whom we had been left had passed away as well.

One day while I was walking on a nearby road, I met a British soldier, who was out on a reconnaissance mission. This particular scene was recalled for me in the first regression, but it wasn't until later that I realized the significance of that meeting. Apparently, the soldier—who is now my husband in this life—and I began a secret relationship, which took place several months before the Allied invasion of Germany. We would meet at night usually, in abandoned barns and the like, and it was after one of these rendezvous that one night I lost my way in the snow, and got picked up by a German patrol.

I had ended up dangerously close to a German encampment, which seemed particularly odd to the Germans as I was discovered there in the middle of the night. Presumably under the suspicion that I had been on a spy mission of some sort, I was brought for questioning before the commandant.

I told them I had been in search of a missing relative and had gotten lost on my return. The commandant didn't believe my story, and I was placed in a cell, uncertain of what my fate would be. I kept holding onto hope that he would soon get bored with the endless questioning and release me, but the commandant didn't seem to feel my story warranted the benefit of the doubt.

In the meantime, I was fretful for the safety of my younger brother, who had no way of knowing what had become of me. I browbeat myself for being so stupid and getting myself in a situation that jeopardized the welfare of someone who depended upon me. I worried about what he would think if I never returned, who would protect him and love him if I wasn't released. I tortured myself with thoughts of what would happen to him without me, now that I had been forced to relinquish responsibility for him.

The commandant, it seems, was a strange and creepy man who had his own particular designs for me. Titillated by the helplessness of my state and his complete control over me, he began to appear in my cell at night looking for sexual favors. Convinced that if I cooperated I may have some chance of freedom, I engaged in this weird liaison, which, though it never raised me above the status of prisoner, was exaggerated in the commandant's mind to a chaste, sincere and perfectly sensible love affair. He often talked about what we would do together after the war, where we would live and such. Then, he would leave me there in my maddening captivity and return to the routine of his military responsibilities.

One night, which I believe to be very near the end of the war, the commandant left the camp on military business. During the night I was attacked and raped by two guards at the camp. When the commandant returned and learned of the attack, he felt betrayed and repelled by the idea of any continued relations with me. He blamed me for having *allowed* the incident to occur, and issued an order for my immediate execution. I was hung the following morning by the two men who had raped me.

The first time I was regressed into this life, I did not realize I had been raped during my incarceration or sexually molested by the commandant. After the hanging, though, I experienced an odd and inexplicable reluctance to leave the earth, while my spirit stood off at a distance looking back at the body of the girl I had been. I felt a strong sense of betrayal, of which I had no understanding. What I did realize then was only that the hesitation I experienced in leaving the earth had to do with the remaining connection I had with my younger brother (Ryan), the regrets I had for having to leave him, and the fears I still felt surrounding the matter of his future well-being. It was an overwhelming mixture of guilt and sadness, a feeling that nothing could ever right the wrong I had caused him.

But of course my son's dramatic entrance into my present life was the second chance I thought during those moments I hovered by Elsa's body, that I would never get. The fretfulness and remorse of those last days of my prior existence insinuated themselves into my current relationship with my son, and metamorphosed into feelings that I didn't deserve to be his mother, that I couldn't be trusted with the overwhelming responsibility I'd been given, and that at any moment I'd be found out, punished and removed from the role of his caretaker.

The fruitless struggle Elsa had made to free herself, an escape which grew more and more unlikely as time went on, transformed itself into the frustrating nightmares that visited me in my dreams, stories of Ryan's loss and the hopelessness of his retrieval, such as the chaotic episode in the London underground.

Other information garnered from these regressions revealed that, though she had feared for the worst, Elsa's little brother *did* survive the war, just as Ryan survived his early struggle for health and stability, an experience which gave me the opportunity to learn how much that outcome had to do with the power of the soul who is Ryan, and how little it had to do with me or Elsa. Ryan is here because he wants to be, and he stays with me because he wants to.

This fact more than anything came through to me after the first time I learned of Elsa. I came home that evening with a feeling of enormous gain and the relief of long-awaited forgiveness, of which Ryan's birth assured me. In the car that night, after we'd taken the baby-sitter home, I looked over at him, sitting in the darkness, his small frame outlined in the light of the traffic. "Thanks for coming back to me," I told him, my eyes brimmed with tears. He looked across the car at me with his old man eyes and his sweet, wise face. "Okay," he said casually, with his usual gift for understatement. "Can we get a donut now?"

***

In my more objective moods, I know it is a blessing that the powerfully willed child I have spawned has always had a complete and unwavering awareness of his own strength of spirit. While I, as a toddler, obligingly submerged mine out of acquiescence to my parents, Ryan has never been the least bit motivated to follow suit. He has never been particularly fussed by anyone's disapproval of his behavior, and while he might find my intervention frustrating to the active quality of his play, he never takes it personally. I don't believe I've ever seen him truly undone by anything. He calmly assesses his capability to handle a particular task or situation, and walks away if he feels he's not up to it. He has the self-possession I have always longed to regain from my own childhood, a conviction which propels him through life with unstaggering sureness.

On the other hand, his willfulness has greatly angered me at times. Since as parents we tend to be sensitive to our children in the areas which were sensitive in our own childhoods, a part of me will firmly entrench itself and match his steadfastness toe to toe. "Why should you get away with what I never could?" I often think, as I put on my strongest and angriest voice for him, while Ryan, composed and unshaken, continues on as if I wasn't even in the room.

"Why are you doing this?" I hollered one day, when we were tussling over one of our more frequent bones of contention. "Because *I am*," he answered, in a matter-of-fact and completely non-defiant tone of voice, as if he were schooling me in the fundamentals of math. He was three years old at the time. I stood looking at him, wondering if in thirty-eight years I had ever had the presence of self to say that to *anyone*.

There have been many moments with Ryan when I have felt more like his child than his mother. I envy the coolness of him, the blissful state of detachment in which he lives. Where is the part of *me* inclined to burst into song in the middle of lunch, or pull faces at my reflection in a nearby glass, that longs to whoop and holler through the house for no more reason than the pure pleasure of being alive? What happened to her?

I remember an afternoon when Ryan was two-and-a-half, and the two of us were in the kitchen making cookies. He was sitting up at the counter on a stool, mixing the dough in a bowl. I was tired and impatient that day, acting out my anger over the flour that had spilled on the floor, and the egg shell that had fallen in the batter. When I'd finished my ranting, I looked over at him. He was staring at me in a way he has, thoughtful and slightly condescending. I apologized for spoiling our time together, and kissed him briefly on the forehead. "I think you need a new mommy," he said after a moment, returning his attention to the cookies.

I was struck by all the levels of wisdom in that statement, the way he seemed to know instinctively that the person to whom he was speaking could be a child sometimes as well as a parent. He was saying both that I needed to be cared for the way a mother cares for her child, and, since I *am* a mother, that I needed to be a different sort of caretaker for myself. It was like him to know these things; it was like him to be so generous in letting me express my frustration, the way the child I was never could.

But a parent shouldn't be a child, and a child shouldn't have to be her parent, my guilty conscience would often remind me. I never felt okay about the bursts of anger that were prone to crash down around this bright and happy child. I was touched, but saddened and worried for the comical blond boy who would look up at me whenever he sensed a storm brewing around him, and tactfully inquire: "Aren't you going to be happy today?"

More than anything I wanted to be a good mother to Ryan. I knew the hardship of growing up with a mother who oftentimes couldn't be counted on for support because she was too absorbed in her own problems. It broke my heart to think I was continuing this legacy at Ryan's expense.

One day when I was feeling particularly down about my nurturing capabilities, I had a meeting with Marion. Seeing how upset I was at the time, she felt that more than uncover a tragic or less than ideal prior parental experience, I needed to witness an experience that would re-acquaint me with the mother I longed to be. The following transcript, of a life which Ryan and I—as the Baroness in the book's title—shared in Amsterdam during the 18th century, is what evolved from that session:

J: Well, there's a country road, and there's a boy who looks to be about 9 or 10 on the side of the road. A carriage has gone by. I'm watching the boy. He's playing and throwing stones and doing cartwheels by the side of the road. This boy is Ryan. I'm walking down the other side of the road. I'm watching him.

M: What is your name?

J: Elise.

M: What is his name?

J: Philip. This is a country house that we have. The house is on a hill and he's running up the hill. On the side of the house there's like an enclosed porch or a large breezeway. He's running through this room, yelping and stuff. (Laughing)   My husband is there.   He comes out laughing at our son.

M: What is your husband's name?

J: Also Philip.

M: Go to the next significant part.   (Hereafter NSP.)

J: We're at a table eating. My son's talking to me about frogs. He's very interested in them, and has studied them; he's telling me about this. He's showing me how their legs move with his hands, and saying something about that. He's very enthusiastic and animated, like he is now. He skips off.

M: NSP.

J: We're by a carriage, and I'm trying to get him to get in the carriage, but he's doing something. We're going out shopping together to get him some clothes. He's very wiry; he never sits still. Very curious. We're by a shop window. There's a boat that he wants. We have an appointment with the clothier. So we go in there. He's getting fitted in a green suit. It's his first man's suit; he's out of little boy's clothes. He has a vest, knee-length pants with tights, and a coat. He's about 14. He's very embarrassed because I'm emotional over the fact that he's getting his first man's suit. But then when the tailor goes away, he squeezes my hand because he understands. He seems to get older and older as I look at him in this outfit, because I'm seeing that now he's moving into another phase, and in my mind I see him at 16 and then 20 as he's growing up. He even has on a wig like the men wear, but I think that's just the way I'm seeing it in my mind.

M: NSP.

J: My husband is dying.[5]   It's nighttime and I'm walking down a hallway. I have on a nightgown; I'm carrying a candle. My son has called me into

---

[5] This was the second time I was regressed into this particular lifetime, which took place between about 1740 and 1793 in Amsterdam. The first

his room, and I'm trying to explain to him what's happening. He wants to know who will take care of us. I tell him, we will take care of each other.

M: NSP.

J: We're back in the country again. It's springtime. I'm sitting up on the top of the hill. There's daffodils all down the hillside. My son has brought me some. I'm still very much in mourning and very depressed. He's too young to know what to say, so he just sits with me for a while. He says he'll go and get me some tea. He leaves. I put my head down into the flowers he's given me and cry.

M: NSP

J: I'm lying on a couch. I think they may be giving me some kind of drugs. I feel very groggy.

M: Are the drugs for your depression?

J: They're to make me sleep. I'm having trouble sleeping. They make me so groggy. I feel I have to get back into life again. My son has been so patient and good to me; he's really lost both his father and his mother. He's away at school and he's coming home. I decide to take an interest in everything he's doing. So I help him with his studies. We talk a lot and get close again.

M: How old is he now?

J: About 15. He really likes history a lot. He likes to talk about what he thinks really happened, you know, behind the scenes sort of. He has a lot of interesting ideas. He thinks a lot like his father.

M: NSP.

J: He's leaving.

M: For where?

---

time I recalled this life, it was revealed that my husband Philip—now my husband Tad—died of rabies which he contracted from the bite of a wolf.

J: *Something to do with the military. Officers' training. He has a uniform on. When he gets in the carriage and rides away, I can't stop crying; my little boy is gone.*

M: *NSP.*

J: *Some sort of parade. My son is in it. He's in uniform.*

M: *What city is the parade in?*

J: *Antwerp.*

M: *NSP.*

J: *He has a girl he's engaged to. She's very doting. They talk about their plans.*

M: *Is he working?*

J: *He's still in the military. We're very wealthy. We don't need to work. He's very happy. It's hard for me to lose him.*

M: *Are they planning to live nearby?*

J: *It's not real close-by; it's near where he's stationed.*

M: *Where is he stationed?*

J: *Onglund.*

M: *Is that in Holland?*

J: *Yes.*

M: *Is there a war going on?*

J: *No.*[6]

---

6 This was a bit confusing. Actually there was a war going on around that time with England (Onglund) from 1780-1784, in which I believe my son was later wounded.

M: NSP.

J: There's some other man, I don't know who it is. I don't know what's going on here.

M: What do you think is going on?

J: I think something has happened to my son. (1-2-3) He's been injured. He's broken his leg.

M: Was that during some military maneuvers?

J: Something fell on his leg. Maybe a cannon. I see something with big black wheels. Looks like a cannon.

M: NSP.

J: He's on crutches.

M: Move ahead to the day of his wedding.

J: He's in uniform. She has a very long train on her dress. I feel very closed out of his life. But I understand that has to happen, and it's not because he doesn't love me. So I've accepted it.

M: Can you go ahead five years and tell me if you have any grandchildren?

J: I have three.

M: Are any of these grandchildren anyone you know now?

J: No.

M: Is your son's wife anyone that you know now?

J: No.

M: I want you to go ahead 10 years and tell me what's happening.

J: I won't be there in ten years.

M: Go to the moment of your death then.

J: I don't seem to be very aware. I must be drugged or something.

M: Tell me when you've died.

J: My son is comforting my daughter.

M: Have you died?

J: Yes.

M: I want you to go to the light, and see if you can meet your Higher self or someone else that you can ask questions of.

J: Yes?

M: Ask whether you were a good mother in that life?

J: You were always a good mother.

M: Ask if there are strengths from that life you can bring into this life to help you to be a good mother.

J: Realize that your son is with you because he wants to be with you.

M: Ask if there's any lesson you should learn from that life that will help you in your mothering in this life.

J: Respect the decision he has made in choosing you for his mother.

M: Any other lesson?

J: Allow yourself to be a mother. It won't hold you back. It will only enhance your life.

M: Any other lessons?

J: Don't look at being a mother as a distraction. It's part of who you are.

M: Any other lesson?

J: Give up trying to control the spirit in him. It's always been there, and it won't go away.

M: Isn't the spirit a good thing?

J: Yes, it's a gift in fact.

M: Ask if there's any other lesson you need to learn before you come back.

J: Let yourself be a mother.

M: Who are you talking to?

J: My dad.

M: As you look back on that life, can you forgive yourself and anyone that may have hurt you?....

***

I have found mothering the most awesome and overwhelming experience of my life. But, it has been necessary for me to realize that the frustrations I have felt from time to time have always been borne out of what I perceive is a departure from some image of motherhood which I relentlessly try to match to the letter. They have never sprung from the failings of my son.

I am an uncompromising taskmaster when it comes to conforming to that image. I must be perfect at this, I tell myself; so much is at stake here. But I fail to remember that I am not the image. I am not the mother who is always calm, always available, always loving and sweet, and Ryan, it is fair to say, knows this better than anyone. He knew it before he arrived, knew what he was getting himself into, so to speak, and *still*, he picked me out of the crowd. Did he pick me because I was perfect? No. He picked me because I was perfect for the job.

It is a curious notion to think that our children choose us as their parents. In our culture, we tend to believe that our children are here because we created them; we made it so. And it is an illusion which causes suffering because it makes us think our children *belong* to us, an illusion helped along by the fact that our children are actually composed of physical matter from our own bodies.

But the physical matter isn't the child we love; it's the soul that has entered it—by that soul's own choice and design. In reality our role as parent is a totally *passive* undertaking; we provide only the opening, the *opportunity* for another soul to enter the world. We don't create our children or the life within them; they do. And if they hadn't believed all along that being our children was the best possible option for them and the growth of the soul within them, they wouldn't be here.

Parenting, it is safe to say is like no other experience on this plane, in it's potential to teach us, in its impact on our lives. We are in awe of our children for being nothing like us; at the same time we are confounded by how much they are *completely* like us. And we will never, ever figure out how they manage to be both at the same time. We think we will always know them implicitly, as if we and our children were of the same mind, but they will always up-end that belief, because they are not us.

I think the hardest lesson we learn about our children is just that: they are not us. They are separate and different, with their own itinerary, their own mission, their own maps. And what's worse, that's the stuff they don't like sharing.

What I believe the physical challenges Ryan experienced in his early life sought to teach me was how to get past the surface of him, how to put my trust in the existence of something that went beyond skin and scars and the stutter of his heart. That experience, coupled with the insights provided through past-life regression, taught me that despairing over the inauspicious caterpillar is pure foolishness; it revealed that all Ryan truly required from his mother was allowance for the butterfly to emerge.

Looking at it today, I know that the struggles I have had—and still have—with Ryan and my role as his mother will survive only for as long as I resist loving him as I originally promised, with all my heart but none of my*self*. I already know the pain of losing him, because I've lost him before. I've tried mistakenly to insulate myself from experiencing this pain again by holding myself back from being Ryan's mother. But, the pain of letting a child go out into the world alone is an inseparable part of the promise and privilege of being his parent.

The most poignant and heart-breaking moment I encountered while recalling my life in Amsterdam, was when I relived my son's departure into military life. Even now I can think back on that moment, see that carriage rolling away down the street, and call up the same measure of pain Elise felt standing there. I don't think it will ever leave me, but then again, I don't believe it's supposed to.

Letting go *is* parenting, for it is not something that happens in a given moment, but something which happens always. It is exactly what the experience of parenthood endeavors to teach us—to give to our children the same respect we owe others: an opportunity to learn, to fail, to try again, to not try—without judgment about how that process should look. Because, it is *their* process.

***

I know now that the struggle I have felt in the role of Ryan's mother hasn't been between him and me, but *within* me, between the part of myself which longs to love him unconditionally, as promised, and the part of me which resists and controls that love out of fear of abandonment—mine of him, that is. Because, that has been my greatest fear all along, not that Ryan would leave me, but that I would distance myself to a point where he would no longer be retrievable.

It was only natural that I would project onto my child the karma of my own childhood. In this and recent lives, abandonment has been a central traumatic issue. Through past-life regression, I have not only plumbed this issue with my father in this life, but through Elsa, who was left by both parents during the last war in Germany, and through Margaret, a young girl in Edwardian England, who committed suicide because she felt abandoned by her father and only remaining parent.

I suppose that's why I dreamed of a connection between Ryan and my father even before my son was born. Just as we are destined to repeat issues from other lives, we are also given opportunities to work out our anxieties toward our parents with our own offspring, who, out of both their own karmic requirements and their own generosity, choose to pick up the thread of our story and play their part.

There is a kind of smug superiority we take on in our role as parents, created perhaps out of our memory of the omniscience which, out of childhood awe, we once bestowed on our own parents. But, being Ryan's mother has been humbling for me in many ways. I don't always have the right answer; I don't always say the right thing. I judge my failings when I don't meet the perfect Mom image—judge it more than he does—and I have found myself explaining these failings to him, and apologizing for being who I am. I forget there are no secrets here. I forget how long he has known and loved me. Like this. Like whatever.

Yes, I have needed to teach him how to use a spoon, and how to work a yo-yo, how to make sure his shoes are on the right feet, and that his shirt isn't on backwards. But, he has much to teach me about life, as well. He has shown me by his example what I need to reclaim from my own childhood—discarded treasures like spontaneity, curiosity, a concentrated sense of self, and a fresh, unspoiled pleasure to be alive.

So, instead of showing him how to be more like me, I find myself often wishing I could unravel myself back to a point in my life where I was perhaps more like him. Whenever I compare our separate and usually opposite reactions to things, I often find his to be the more centered and reasonable of the two. Where I might be indignant about the school bus that left him waiting forty minutes in the cold, Ryan is calm and accepting. "Aren't you upset about this?" I ask him. "No," he answers, knitting his brows, "would it make the bus come if I was?"

I notice constantly how he accepts each of his friends at face value, and doesn't judge them for how they act or who they are, while I am rushing to criticize and disapprove. Is judgment and cynicism what I want my son to learn, I ask myself, when here he is so open to what the world has to offer him? Or, is it I who must learn from him to give life a chance?

What I must remember above all else, now, is that the give and take between parent and child flows both ways, and that the experience of parenthood is really just an *exchange* between two souls who have chosen to help one another make a journey through life. Because, like all children born to this world, Ryan arrived, open-hearted, his arms spilling over with gifts.

To F.T.B

Then we w
where the
ma   ic like
and shi   re as counti
And   ut words to th
th   uld only be something l   s
than what they are.
If I tried to say--
e this coil our hands make, hear this
catch of our breaths on the clutch
of the hill, sleep this night of
calibrated dreaming--
It would need the rush
of a whole new language,
one that is primeval and secret,
tempered, inviolate,
and at all times silent,
like a tree being swallowed
in the throat of a forest.

Love, JBB

"Alone Together"

Chapter Five

Alone Together

When I first became engaged to the man who later became my husband, I thought I knew him well. At the time, I assumed, quite incorrectly, that our instinctive sort of ease with one another ensured a smooth and easy journey ahead, as if compatibility automatically implied the absence of challenge for us. We would always understand each other, I thought, read each other's feelings with this high-calibre sensory perception we'd been given towards each other, and behave accordingly with complete sensitivity and appropriateness.

Ironically, it has probably been allegiance to that expectation which has created for me my occasional disappointment with him; marriage to that image, not marriage to the man, which has challenged me the most over time.

It is surprising, in fact, as I look at us now, after nine years of marriage, how perfect my choice of husband really was. It amazes me that I somehow recognized how well-suited we were, when, in reality I didn't know him very well at all then. In fact, part of what I've come to learn over the years is that getting to know each other is what we've really been about, he and I—two people who are forever trying to learn and appreciate who the other one really is.

My husband is not an easy man to read. It amuses me, sometimes, the number of people who get him totally wrong. And yet, for as much as I think *I* know him, he will always, always surprise me. I suppose it will take me a long time to learn I can't second guess him. Just when I think I have him all perfectly contained in my mind, he'll prove how limited that definition of him is, walking in the door with a book I would never expect him to buy, making an observation which is completely untypical, or laughing at something I would never dream he'd find funny.

What surprises me most about Tad, though, is that he's there; he endures. I keep wondering when he's going to wake up and realize I'm really not worth all this attention and trouble. But the next day, and the next week and the next year, there he is, still forgiving me my faults, still loving and appreciating me, still trying to understand what makes me tick. What does he see when he looks at me, I wonder, and how far from reality is the person I see when I look at him?

I waiver from believing that loving him means having the capability of seeing right through him to the core, straight through all the nonsense and the smokescreens and the barriers to the center and heart, to believing that loving him is precisely what keeps me from ever knowing him at all. Perhaps it is only some mad mix of perceptions I hold in my mind, a collection of my own faulty interpretations of what he says and does, which may come close, but never touch the truth, never approach the realness of him.

But then sometimes, I get this sense that it is the *closeness* which blinds me, that only with distance does my focus seem to sharpen. Whenever my husband and I are apart, I often get, not a different, but what feels like a more correct understanding of him. I feel that I arrive at some higher level of perception of who he is and why we ended up together, a revelation I decide must be communicated once we reunite.

Mentally, I formulate this revelation—whatever it may be—into concrete thoughts and sentences, but somehow even that process always makes it seem less true. It is perhaps hours or days before he comes in the door, before I even get the opportunity to talk to him. And then, when he enters the house, tired from the office or his business trip, this kind of communication suddenly seems impossible, as I watch him frown and flip through the mail, trying to make the transition into the world of his wife and children, squinting in the light from the kitchen, as if even his eyesight must adjust.

As he reenters the life we share together from his other worldly existence, he seems somehow blurred, distorted by its effects, and when I look up at him from the dinner preparations, the child-tending or the telephone, I notice something altogether unfamiliar in him, something which—in arriving at these thoughts I'd been safekeeping—I either forgot about or overlooked.

Is it the wearing off of the recent distance between us that I see in that moment, or the difference between who he is and who I think he is? Whatever the reason, we both feel disoriented, and test the waters with each other for the next several hours or days. Are you still the same person you were when we parted last, we seem to want to know, slightly begrudging one another all the moments and things we experienced during our separation?

It's an odd sort of thing, something unnameable really, but we both feel it, and know its effects. It makes us grouchy and defensive of the privacy we must now relinquish. For two people who are so well-suited, so basically content to be together, it has always made me wonder why we must make this strange acclimation to one another after every time we've been apart.

It doesn't seem to be an issue of trust. It's not a matter of our having to account for our time alone to one another. Nor is it an issue of needing more space from each other, because I have never known anyone with whom I like to be around so much. I have never felt bored or in need of space from my husband. Even in the middle of a heated argument, when my husband feels the need to walk out of the room or the house to cool off, some part of me is sad to see him leave. Some part of me—despite the consuming anger of the moment—is preoccupied with the emptiness that comes from being separated from him and the apprehension that maybe he won't come back.

***

In all the lifetimes I have uncovered during the process of past-life regression therapy—in which he has figured—my husband and I have been prematurely separated by either death or desertion. That's not to say that there probably haven't been a number of lifetimes together in which we have lived happily on to a ripe old age, but separation has become a sort of recurrent theme for us, and the anxiety that has lingered on from this repeated scenario has left its emotional residue on our current life together.

When I first met my husband and experienced that feeling of familiarity and "knowingness" about him, it was because I did know him, and have known him under many different circumstances across many different centuries. It was a sixth sense about him that I have always felt, but never quite knew how to articulate.

No love, after all is new; it's, instead, part of a continuing, remembered energy. The sort of clean, clear optimism we feel when we find a new lover or hold a new baby in our arms is really new *hope*. Here's our chance to rectify the past, we seem to say; here's our opportunity to set everything right. At that point we are able to see and feel nothing but the pure energy of the bond we share with this individual, and the intent of the promise we made to come together.

But the seeds of what we haven't forgiven soon begin to root themselves. We find ourselves getting hurt, feeling disappointed, having arguments about seemingly unimportant though emotionally-charged things. Soon our disillusionment and confusion begin to restore the walls we began building between ourselves and our loved ones lifetimes before, walls of which we can't even consciously recall the design or intent.

For my husband and I, our particular wall has been built out of the anxieties of separation and our inability to forgive one another for having failed to simply accept without question or analysis each opportunity we have had to be together. For failing each time to follow our hearts.

I recalled, for instance, a lifetime in Amsterdam when my husband (then and now) died rather young after having contracted rabies. The woman I was then suffered for many years with the anger and anxiety of having been left with two small children, and the guilt which resulted from feeling she should have done something to prevent the death. At the end of that regression I was directed to ask my Higher self what understanding of my current marriage I could gain from recalling this lifetime. The answer was to remember that my husband loves me no matter what, and that the troubles which exist between us from time to time stem from the fact that because we have so often parted, neither of us truly believes the other really loves him.

***

All of us, in some way or other, find curious the notion of having a so-called "soul-mate" in life. Some will believe it to be a partner not just for life but for many lives, someone to whom we are united again and again through time. Before they arrive, however, we tend to get very anxious. How will we recognize them, we wonder? Will we somehow miss the opportunity to share our life with them if we don't pay close attention?

It is needless to worry about the mechanics of such things. Unconsciously, we know where we're headed all the time. It is the ego—the personality—which is always crying out for the road maps. The ego is like the child in the back seat who keeps asking her parent: "Are we there yet?" The best we can do is hold within the desire for love and the belief that we always meet up in life with precisely whom we are supposed to, exactly when we're ready for them.

There are many common misconceptions about the soul-mate relationship. One is the notion that we keep coming back together lifetime after lifetime because we keep getting it wrong. It is not the "wrongness" of a relationship, but the "rightness" of it which draws us to one another again and again.   It is the enduring power of love that attracts, not memories of bitter moments once shared.

The karma, or what manifests itself as trouble spots in a relationship, does not operate as a potentially destructive force against which we are powerless, but as a reminder of the imbalances between two people which they now desire to correct.   Karma, after all, is really no more than fuel for the evolution of the soul.

The second somewhat misguided line of thinking goes something like this: I keep having failed relationships because I haven't met the *right* person.   Once I meet that person, all my troubles will be over and we'll both live happily ever after.

Ironic as it may seem, there is probably more *possibility* of discord within a soul-mate relationship because, first of all, there has been more opportunity for karma to develop there.   Secondly, there is expressed commitment between soul-mates—before entering life even—to help one another to evolve.   It is in fact, the whole point of the union.   When stress areas appear within a marriage or love relationship, it doesn't indicate mismatch or wrongness in the relationship so much as it indicates the areas where we personally need to seek change.   We don't like to hear this of course, but it is by providing challenge that the soul-mate relationship demonstrates its true worth, and the existence of discord does not make the relationship or the choice of partner any less *perfect*.

Experience on this plane is, after all, dualistic (i.e., positive and negative), and so anything that is part of that experience—like a relationship—will naturally assume dualistic properties.   This is not a bad thing, remember, since the purpose of being here in the first place is to evolve, and duality is the tool through which we do that.   Conflict then has positive potential.   We can look at its presence as a joint commitment, made out of love, by two people who wish to embellish through experience the bond they share.

So many people experience feelings of regret at having involved themselves in a relationship that fails, believing they have wasted precious time and energy on something that didn't pan out.   All relationships, failed or successful, evolve us, put us in a different place than we were before they began.   Sometimes the separation itself, rather than the relationship, is the real learning ground or karmic challenge.   And so, just as we choose the partners with whom we will endure, we will also choose the ones from whom we will eventually part.   In short, we gain from all life experiences, more often the negative ones, and so, regardless of the result, we should be thankful for all people with whom we have shared love.

***

Seeing the people we love under different circumstances, such as what is experienced through past-life regression therapy, has a startling impact all its own, perhaps more than the experience of seeing one's own self change from lifetime to lifetime. It's interesting how the properties that make us who we are can distill themselves into the images and flashes of memory that appear in the mind during the regression process.

Tad always came through quite sharply for me, that quality which makes him *him*, was always distinct, no matter what the sex, the age, dress or behavior. Each of us seems to have his own particular strain of energy which makes us who we are, and makes us recognizable to the people who love us, no matter how much we alter our personality throughout time.

An example of this is a lifetime I spent with him at the turn of the 18th century. Here, I recognized a part of him which is largely hidden within the person he is now. My husband generally strikes people as a very intense and serious-minded individual. On the one hand, he comes across as someone who is a bit self-conscious and very reluctant to draw attention to himself. But underneath that reserve, is an individual with the most irreverent sense of humor I know, and a man who has a propensity to do and say the outrageous. He's the one I came across one day in 1699:

J: I see a man with a cape on. A Three Musketeer *kind of dress. He's involved in some kind of game. He's throwing some things that look like bowling pins with long skinny necks. He's acting very silly, dancing around and making jokes. He's throwing a javelin. I'm trying to get a sense of him. I think he might be my husband but I'm not sure.*

M: What's his name?

J: Darran

M: What year are we in?

J: 1699.

M: What country?

J: England.

M: What is your name?

J: *Elizabeth.*

M: *What are you wearing.*

J: *A rather fancy dress. I'm a lady-in-waiting. We're at a castle.*

M: *Can you give me the name of the castle?*

J: *Albemarle.*[7]

M: *What does Darran do?*

J: *(Laughing.) I can't imagine this, but I keep getting court jester.*

M: *That's what you count on. Are you married to him?*

J: *No.*

M: *How old are you?*

J: *About 17.*

M: *How old is Darran?*

J: *20.*

M: *What kind of relationship do you have with Darran?*

J: *We're friends.*

M: *Go to the next significant part. (Hereafter NSP.)*

J: *He's performing. Doing a juggling act.*

---

[7] This probably refers to the castle of the Duke of Albemarle, or George Monck, an English general, who was the chief architect of the Restoration of Charles II of the Stuart Monarchy to the throne in 1660. King William III, who was monarch at the time of this regression, was the nephew of Charles II.

M: You're smiling. What makes you smile?

J: I can't imagine him in this capacity.

M: You mean your present husband?

J: Yes. I'm sitting on a bench. There's a lot of people around watching. There seems to be a king or a high lord of some sort there. [8]

M: NSP.

J: I'm standing out by a parapet. I'm talking to Darran. We're sort of courting. He's talking about his job. He's saying how easy it is, and how much he likes to make people laugh. He says that when he has everybody laughing, he feels like everybody likes him. He says there's no other way to capture that feeling. He's very high-strung in some ways. He never stops performing or posing. He never stands still.

M: NSP.

J: I'm sitting in a window. He knocks on the door. He's not supposed to be up there in the ladies' chambers. He says he goes wherever he wants, and no one pays any attention to him. He's laughing and says, 'They think I'm a eunuch.'

M: NSP.

J: We're outside on part of the grounds. We're rolling down the hill and we're laughing. It's a very steep hill. Every time I stop myself, he gives me a shove so I keep rolling. We're rolling around and laughing really hard and pushing each other. We can't stop laughing. We're just acting crazy. He never stops acting crazy.

M: NSP.

J: I think we're getting married. He's got this very formal coat on, and then when he turns around he's got this animal tail hanging out the back. Everyone's laughing. He says, 'I couldn't do it straight'.

---

[8] This was King William III.

M: What are you wearing?

J: I have on a cream colored or yellow dress. It's brocaded.

M: Tell me what happens when the ceremony goes on.

J: The wedding is outside in the garden. Either that or it's a very open kind of church. It seems to be very bright.

M: Is there a wedding party?

J: No just some witnesses.

M: NSP.

J: We're running around the bedroom laughing. He's throwing water at me.

M: Do you make love?

J: Yes, lots of times.

M: Is it satisfying to both of you?

J: Yes.

M: NSP.

J: I have all this crinoline material around me. It's a dress. It might be for a coronation or some kind of ceremony.

M: Who's coronation?

J: King William? Queen Anne.[9]

M: NSP.

---

[9] This was actually the coronation of Queen Anne, who took over the throne from her cousin William. Her coronation did entail some major changes in court personnel.

J: I'm waiting outside a cathedral. I have on a red velvet cape, and this crinoline dress, which is very uncomfortable.

M: Who are you waiting for?

J: Darran.

M: Does he come?

J: No, I go inside to wait. It's really cold.

M: What happens?

J: He doesn't show up.

M: Why not?

J: He's gone. He's left the country.

M: Why?

J: Something that has to do with the change in the court. [10]

M: He didn't tell you ahead of time?

J: No.

M: Couldn't he?

J: I don't know.

M: Was he abducted?

J: No.

[10] It was customary for the comic, or jester, to follow the court. With the death of William III, and the ascent of his estranged sister-in-law Anne to the throne, major changes in personnel were likely to occur, leaving Darran out of favor with the incoming court. As I understood it better later, it seems he had little career options at this point, and went to France to join a traveling minstrel show, not the life he imagined I should be living.

M: *I'll count to three and you'll know why he didn't tell you. (1-2-3.)*

J: *He didn't want to hurt me.*

M: *Didn't it hurt you that he left without telling you?*

J: *He thought I'd be better off without him.*

M: *I want you to go ahead five years and tell me what's happening in that life.*

J: *I'm married to someone else.*

M: *Was your marriage annulled?*

J: *Yes.*

M: *Who are you married to now?*

J: *John of Asquith.*

M: *Tell me about him.*

J: *He's an officer to the queen.*

M: *How old are you now?*

J: *23.*

M: *Do you and John have any children?*

J: *A boy Robert.*

M: *Do you know either John or Robert from your present life?*

J: *I don't think so.*

M: *Are you happy with John?*

J: *He takes good care of me.*

M: *Go ahead another five years and tell me what's happening.*

J: *It's a masquerade ball.*

M: *Where is it?*

J: *At the palace.*

M: *NSP.*

J: *Darran is at the masquerade ball. I know it's him because he has a tail sticking out of the back of his coat.*

M: *NSP.*

J: *I'm talking to Darran. He says, he left because he knew he couldn't make me happy. And I say, isn't that a bit ironic? He says, I could make you laugh, but I couldn't make you happy. I say, then you don't know anything about what makes me happy.*

M: *Do you still love him?*

J: *Yes. Very much.*

M: *What happens?*

J: *Nothing happens.*

M: *Go ahead 10 years and tell me what's happening.*

J: *I have a daughter. Her name is Sarah. She seems to be about seven or eight.*

M: *Do you get along well with your husband and your children?*

J: *Yes.*

M: *Do you love them all?*

J: *I seem to be very attached to the little girl.*

M: *Is she anyone in this life?*

J: Not yet.

M: I want you to go to the moment of your death, and tell me what's happening.

J: I'm in a bed and there's a man leaning over me.

M: Who is it?

J: My husband John.

M: What's he saying?

J: He's trying to tuck me in.

M: What are you dying of?

J: I have a fever.

M: I want you to go to the moment of your death, and tell me when you've died.

J: I feel reluctant to leave my daughter.

M: How old are you now?

J: About 47.

M: Go to the moment of your death, and tell me when you've died.

J: I seem to be dead.

M: Go toward the light and tell me when you find someone to talk to.

J: Darran's there.

M: What does he say to you?

J: I was very wrong to leave you.

M: Is he sorry?

J: Yes.

M: Does he ask you to forgive him?

J: Yes.

M: Do you?

J: Yes.

M: Ask him if he has any message to give you from that life that you need to bring to this life.

J: We need to laugh more.

M: What else?

J: He says I needed to forgive him.

M: Didn't you forgive him?

J: He's suggesting that I hadn't before now.

M: Is there any other message?

J: No.

M: Can you forgive anyone else in that life who may have wronged you?

J: Yes.

M: Is there someone you need to ask forgiveness of?

J: My second husband.

M: Have you asked his forgiveness?

J: Yes. He says he knew all along that I didn't love him.

M: Can you send light and love to everyone you knew in that lifetime?

J: Yes.

M: I want you to bring back from that life the feeling of being loved and loving in return, and having fun in your loving....

***

For as much as other relationships have been a challenge and a learning experience, no other relationship in my life has tested me as consistently—or as well—as the one I share with my husband.

It is easy to have knowledge of the importance of compassion and tolerance in a relationship, to *say* that one must not criticize or hold back love from another because he is not like you or because he makes separate choices, likes different things or feels another way than you do. It is another to master that, instinctively and constantly in each moment you are together. This is the lesson my husband and my marriage to him provide me, and while I may grumble a good deal from time to time about the difficulty of the test, I am eternally thankful for the opportunity to sit down and take it.

For me the test has been—and I believe this is true in any love relationship—to not get caught up on the differences between my husband and myself. There is no doubt that I was drawn to him—just as we are all drawn to the ones we love—because he reflects something of who I am, a kindred spirit in other words. But the purpose of this reflection has been to provide me with an objective form from which to evolve and better understand myself and all that I've experienced in life. It has not been a form from which to shape him into something more to my liking.

Admittedly, I have put great effort from time to time into getting my husband to think like I do, or to appreciate the same things I do, to value what I value and share in my enthusiasm about it. I have to say I have been annoyed and frustrated at him for repeatedly refusing to do so. But then, why should I have ever expected him to in the first place? Why should being my husband obligate this man I married to view all of life and its experiences as I do?

Growing up, I learned as we perhaps all did that the goal of a healthy marriage is for its two partners to become as one. Our socialization has made us believe that relationships which cannot achieve this assimilation of spirit are failed and incompatible ones. But surely, renunciation of the self is not the pathway toward greater harmony in any relationship. Surely it's not the objective to erase the differences between us, but to learn to celebrate them.

As I said before, I have stared at my husband in certain moments and been completely unsure of who he really is. Is he this man I chose for being at once a contrast to and a reflection of who *I* am, or is he some fellow traveller through time, whose journey has sometimes been fortuitously placed alongside my own?

The answer I have learned is both. The former is but a component of the latter, and the ongoing challenge for me is to always allow my husband to *experience* both, not just the part of himself he shares with me.

I think physical separation from a loved one—the kind experienced many lifetimes over by my husband and me—has really been just a reminder of something much more important than the separation itself, a metaphor for this truth we must all come to finally face: that true love is joy for the separateness between us as much as it is joy for the connection that holds us fast.

***

Perhaps it is idealistic to think that the two of us are soul-mates who meet again and again across the line of time, dividing out of and reuniting into one another's arms, forever attached by a bright thread of love that holds us together. But my heart tells me that's the way it is.

And in the process, my heart has learned that the odd sensation I get in that moment I first look up at him as he comes through the door is no more than recognition, a momentary *tuning in* of immortal memory to this soul with whom I have shared so much time. It notices everything that is new, recalls everything that is the same, and from somewhere down deep, it calls out to him: "So it's you again. Who are you this time, and how long will you be staying?"

Part Two:

Aspects of the Self

"Looking Back"

Chapter Six

Looking Back

When I first began to have back problems twenty years ago, I was told by the orthopedist and chiropractors who examined me at the time, that there were certain physical anomalies that could be responsible for my trouble, namely a mild curvature of the spine at the point between my shoulder blades, and a longer than usual vertebra at the base of my neck. Having said that, however, they also advised me that these physical deviations were too minor to perpetrate the kind of non-stop discomfort with which I was living.

At the time it was exasperating to receive information such as this. I kept thinking there must be something they were missing, that there must be something simple I could do, or not do, to control the constant pain and tightness in my back. The feeling of frustration continued for many years, however, because the unnamed cause of the problem seemed to forever elude me. Then at some point, I don't remember when exactly, I began to realize that there was a very large and powerful emotional component to the situation.

It is for many a troublesome notion that physical ailment can be rooted in the mind. But through the years I have come to understand more and more how profound a connection there actually is between the mental and the physical. I think some of us find this idea disconcerting, because it seems to imply that an illness produced by the mind and not by the body, or the external environment, is somehow unreal, a kind of ruse created by the victim in order to garner sympathy and caring from others. But the concept to me says merely that communication between the mind and body is absolute, and that what the mind believes—on either a conscious or unconscious level—will be manifested in the body.

Physical illness is our brainchild, the alarm which resounds back to us—in poetic metaphor—all of the unfortunate misconceptions we hold about ourselves. Hence, the person who is experiencing some learning about the giving or receiving of love, may develop heart problems; the person who carries a belief that she cannot handle responsibility might experience some impairment of the shoulders or arms. Our ailments are *literal* translations of every notion we carry about ourselves—that we are weak, unlovable, untrustworthy, rotten to the core—and what we try to hide from the world at large because we are so deeply ashamed.

It is the conviction about our imperfections which is illusory here, not the illness itself. We sometimes get confused on this point, and it is, I believe, why many find the notion of self-created illness so troubling. To say "it's all in your mind," they interpret, is, in effect, to say, "you aren't really sick." But disease and pain and illness are real and meaningful aspects of the dualistic experience we are currently living. That they exist, does not, however, point to our powerlessness and susceptibility on this planet. The presence of illness in our experience indicates simply that each of us holds within the supreme capability to convert any and all beliefs—be they negative or positive—into reality.

***

In my own case, I am aware of at least seven lives (not including the present) in which some trauma to the back region was experienced. It seems that just as we fall back into the same *emotional* patterns we have dealt with in past lives, we fall back into relative physical patterns as well, mainly because the latter is purely a reflection of the former.

Parts of the body, then, become metaphors or seats of karmic experience, which allows us to create—for the sake of evolvement—a physical manifestation of some thought or emotion, e.g., "I don't want to *see* this," may translate itself into cataracts, blindness or other vision impairment. Similarly, the ability to see all sides of an issue, to yield or bend with ease, to feel unthreatened and safe from opposing viewpoints might find expression in a flexible and healthy spine, just as resistance to alternative ideas and bullheadedness might be associated with a rigid and tense one.

Alleviating physical pain by means of past-life regression therapy is, then, really a two-part issue. Bringing memory of prior physical injury to the conscious mind, and releasing it from its constant struggle to express itself from within the confines of the unconscious mind is the initial step. But, identifying and relieving the pockets of emotion *associated with* the physical injury is the other, more pertinent part of the process.

In my own case, I found recurring issues of abandonment, undeserved punishment and wrongful death, lack of support, powerlessness and the inability to forgive surfacing again and again throughout past-life memories related to my back. In addition to two lives in which spinal injury was relevant, namely Margaret (Chapter One), who was crippled in a fall from a horse, and Elsa (Chapter Four) who was hung, these emotional issues were also relevant in three other lives, which I'll mention briefly: Josiah, a slave who was wrongfully accused of stealing his master's money and hung on a cross; Jason, a serf, who was punished for not being able to meet his rents through a rather macabre process in which he was made to push a mill wheel while carrying increasing weights of stone on his back; and Gisette, a young French woman, whose father hung her by the wrists from a pole, which he had shoved out a high tower window, until she promised she would stop her clandestine meetings with a man her father found unsuitable for her. She subsequently starved herself to death in a nunnery, where her father sent her after she had twice tried to run away with her lover.

Though not terribly interesting when taken at face value, the back trauma endured in these lifetimes were all seated with feelings of failure, loss of support, powerlessness, anger, frustrated goals and loss of autonomy, so that, logically speaking, an arousal of these particular emotions for me now, causes tension in the physical area with which those emotions associate themselves.

When I arrived at the end of my life as Gisette, I was told that I would not have felt it necessary to kill myself if I had been able to forgive my father. Forgiveness of the self and others became a recurring theme throughout the entire process of my past-life therapy, but it seems best highlighted through the discussion of this chapter, because I discovered along the way that my back trouble was simply an objective reflection of an historic inability to let go of past transgressions and remain *flexible* to alternative viewpoints.

A past-life experience which illustrates this more clearly is one which occurred to me at the end of the last century. I initially became aware of this individual, whose name was François Tremaine, while meditating on the cause of some pain I had in my right shoulder and neck. The next time I went to see Marion, we explored the life of this man more closely to discover what relevance it bore to my back problems:

J: I'm in a desert area. There's a sea nearby. Maybe the Mediterranean. I'm a soldier. I have a hat on with a chin strap. I'm coming out of my quarters. I'm just looking around; I'm standing by a railing. I have on a white uniform and high boots. I go into my quarters and I take my hat off. It's white with gold trim. There's a flap down the back like the French Foreign Legion. I'm a major. I sit down at my desk. I have some kind of campaign and I'm deciding which men to take with me. It's 1888. I'm about 30 or 32. My father was an officer and he raised me to be an officer. He trained me not to have any emotions. And I don't.

M: *What is your name?*

J: *François Tremaine.*

M: *What is happening now?*

J: *I'm trying to organize my men. Some of the troops are native to this country, not many. I've decided not to take them because I'm afraid they may be traitors. I don't tell my men much about what we're going to do, but I've received orders to go and investigate a possible rebellion. Some of the men don't seem to be very well-equipped. They are too homesick or too afraid.*

M: *What does that have to do with their not being well equipped?*

J: *If their emotions get in the way, they won't be prepared for battle. There's one soldier in particular who comes and visits me every once in a while. He's very homesick and doesn't feel he should be here. I feel in time he'll get used to it.*

M: *Is he French or native?*

J: *French. I guess he has....there's a letter that's come for him, and I'm holding it for him. I don't think he can handle reading it; his wife and child are very ill, it seems. My father has taught me that when you're on assignment, you have no personal life. When I was younger, my father used to....I'm not sure whether it was punishment or part of my training. There were a number of endurance tests. Standing at attention out in the sun for hours on end. There was something about walking on heated rocks so I could endure pain. When I was about 14, I stopped reacting, and that was when he thought I was ready. He wanted me to be a perfect soldier.*

There was a servant boy, Syrian, whom I was friendly with when I was about six. He was the son of one of the servants in the house, and we played together. My father wanted me to have contempt for the Syrians and realize I was above them. He had this boy whip me so that I would learn contempt for him. My father convinced me that the humiliation I felt from the beating was because the boy wasn't my equal.

M: Go to the next significant part. (Hereafter NSP.)

J: I'm on my horse. I'm prepared for battle. I think this is a surprise attack. It's designed to discourage any further insurgency. My orders are to massacre the village. We're charging across the desert. All the people outside the village are fleeing. Many of them are just trampled.

M: NSP.

J: It's quiet now. We've just gone into the heart of the village to look around. It seems like everyone is dead. I don't feel victorious. I just feel like I did what I was told to do.

M: NSP.

J: I'm falling off my horse. I have a knife in my back.

M: Who put the knife in your back?

J: One of the rebels.

M: Are you dying?

J: I'm hanging upside down. Maybe my foot is caught in the stirrups. I'm trying to see what's going on. All these people come rushing out of the buildings where they were lying in wait. Soldiers are scattering everywhere. I have a hard time breathing. My throat is full of blood. A man comes and takes me down, one of the rebels. I think my foot is still caught. He stabs me several times in the chest. He slits my throat. I'm dead. I'm watching the horse take my body down the road.

M: Where are you?

J: Just above, watching. I don't feel much emotional connection to any of this.

M: NSP.

J: There's all these people filing into heaven. Rows and rows of them.

M: Are these the people you were responsible for killing?

J: Yes. There's a spirit in a white robe who tells me I have to wait for all these people to pass before I can come in. I see that soldier with his wife and his child. They must have died from their illness. I feel very envious of him.

M: Why?

J: Because I don't have anyone who loves me.

M: Stay with the emotion. What does it feel like?

J: Like I live alone in the world. There are all these people around me and I have no connection to any of them. I feel like a machine. Some of the people look at me, but most of them don't. I wish they would just look at me. It would make me feel like I'm real.

M: What would you like to tell them?

J: I didn't want to be the way I was. I felt I had no choice.

M: Can you ask their forgiveness?

J: Yes.

M: Can you forgive yourself?

J: I feel I was very weak and stupid.

M: Is the being in white ready to talk to you?

J: Yes.

M: Ask him what was the lesson you were to learn from that life.

J: To recognize my goodness.

M: What about standing up for what you believe is right?

J: I was just a boy. I didn't have much choice.

M: Ask the being if you are forgiven.

J: He says I was forgiven before I came. He says it's not up to him to forgive. He says you must forgive yourself. He says, what do you think you did wrong?

M: What do you say?

J: I say I was cold and unfeeling. He says it was a price you paid because you wanted your father's love. How is that so different from any other boy?

M: What do you respond?

J: I see that my motive was possibly acceptable; I didn't have a bad motive.

M: Ask him if there's anything you are to do in this life to make up for the way you were in that life.

J: I'm to be a spokesperson.

M: For what?

J: The importance of forgiveness.

M: Now that you have talked this over, do you think you can forgive yourself?

J: Yes.

M: Ask the being if one of the lessons of this life is to become more aware of your feelings.

J: He says you're doing that now.

M: Is it one of your assignments in this life?

J: He says that was inevitable.

M: Do you feel clear that you have forgiven yourself and that the others have forgiven you?

J: Yes.

***

Though it was always surprising to me how familiar the personalities I uncovered during the PLT process were, François Tremaine was *particularly* memorable. There was so much pent up emotion in this individual, I felt an overwhelming desire to weep throughout the regression. And I *did* cry—a lot, as I remember—and almost without any forethought, through most of the regression itself and all the way home in the car. It was like some plug had popped somewhere inside me, and this torrent of emotion was exploding out of it.

Whenever I experience back pain now—which occasionally I still do—it is to François Tremaine that I often turn for insight. I try to focus my mind on the release of that vast swell of emotion, and usually, whatever is behind the present pain becomes clearer. I would say that historically, my tendency toward back trouble has had more to do with denial of emotion than expression of it, some feeling or other I'd been sweeping under the rug or allowing to build up without acknowledgement. Once that feeling is addressed, the back discomfort seems to fade.

The most important change this experience effected, however, was what it taught me about the powers of self-healing. Because I saw what past-life regression could accomplish in easing my back troubles, I began to approach any and every physical ailment, large or small, from the viewpoint: How did I create this? In an effort to identify the thought pattern originally responsible for the pain or illness, I learned to methodically backtrack through all the emotions the particular ailment seemed to set off in me. Was it anger, frustration, helplessness, despair? Then, once I felt I had a full inventory of which alarms were sounding, I'd try to determine what thought was setting them off.

For example, about a year ago I strained my shoulder rather badly. It was giving me a lot of trouble, and at one point was so bad I couldn't even breathe deeply or stand up straight without experiencing a shooting pain across my back.

At the time I'd been going through some big decisions regarding the publishing of this book. I was feeling frustrated and helpless, questioning why I was even trying to make a career of writing in the first place. I was also aware of some guilt and feelings of responsibility to my husband and children, who had been very patient, and I thought, had sacrificed much over the years in order to give me the creative space I needed.

One morning while I was meditating about this and sort of mentally zeroing in on the pain in my shoulder and these emotions of helplessness, I suddenly had a flashback of myself, struggling to be born into this life. My shoulder was wedged in the birth canal in some way and as I lay there, lodged, my neck cramped, I started to panic about going any further. What I said to myself over and over in those moments of impasse—and apparently what I have repeated to myself frequently throughout this life—was: "I can't do this. I can't do this by myself."

Here again, the question might arise: was this real memory or simple metaphor created out of the situation? All I can say is that for me it was pure revelation; it was as if someone inside my head had just screamed *bingo!* In that moment I had located a thought pattern which as far as I'm concerned underlies much of the anxiety I have ever outwardly expressed through my back, and because it was there in my mind *before* this life even began, I knew that it was karmic in origin. Where it was initially learned, I can't say, but I do know the power and impact it's had, and the conviction with which it speaks, as it reminds me over and over again, that without the support of others, I can accomplish nothing in life.

Past-life regression therapy and meditation are not by any stretch the only methods of self-healing available to us. Some will swear by the use of positive affirmation, a sort of canceling out of negative thought through a repetitive barrage of corresponding positive thought. For instance, I might address my own episodes of back pain with phrases like: "I have all the support I need," or "I can achieve whatever I desire" in order to eventually retrain my mind to react less negatively as it tries to evaluate what it's experiencing.

Personally, I have found the use of white light in healing particularly effective, and its implementation simple and accessible. It involves mentally tapping into God-consciousness energy by envisioning a circle of white light around whatever is in need of healing or protection. I have gotten rid of warts this way, various infections, flu, and even menstrual irregularities.

A state of quiet concentration is perhaps preferable, when tapping into white light or God-energy, but acknowledgement of its source and belief in its powers to heal are essential. It works because it replaces fear and vulnerability with feelings of well-being and safety. Its uses are endless, and I have called upon white light to protect myself and my loved ones from accident and harm, my house from damage, and my finances and other belongings from loss. I also have never known it to fail.

***

When we are honest and clear-minded, we are all capable of seeing what traps we continually set for ourselves. For as long as we believe that's where we belong, we will remain within the control of our negative habits and thought patterns. At the root of all this seemingly masochistic behavior, is simply the inability to forgive ourselves for past mistakes, and the conviction that we don't deserve to be either happy or loved, healthy, successful or free. Behind our ceaseless prattle and judgment and criticism of others, stands the person we really find hardest to accept, love, and forgive, the person we confront in the mirror every day.

Loving the self is our ultimate and overriding lesson on the Earth plane, and the difficulty of our lives, past and present, is precisely a measure of how much we fail to do this. It is actually our failure to love and accept ourselves—no matter what—which scars the soul and forces us to return again and again into disturbing and violent experiences that in reality should have no relevance. We are always free to eliminate suffering from our life, but letting go of what we feel is deserved recompense for past mistakes is somehow so difficult for us.

The importance of PLT is that it affords us the opportunity to bring to the conscious mind the roots of all the negative programs we run and re-run constantly in our heads. If we can achieve understanding, and forgive the pitfalls of previous existences, we may no longer feel compelled to punish *our selves*, and the destructive tapes that play in our heads, oftentimes unbeknownst to us, will cease to run.

Illness, after all, feeds off the language of illusion, the language of "I can't" and "I'm too old" and "I'm not strong or well enough." We need to adopt a new language, a new logic. One which says: If I created this body, then I created this illness. If I created this illness, then I can heal it. One which, in effect, says: *I can do anything.*

To even let go for one minute of our sense of victimization, of our being at the mercy of illness and disease, to say: "I dare to do something to erase this from my experience" is an enormous step forward.

I have come a long way in healing my back, and it is true that since past-life regression, I no longer experience the sort of relentless pain and discomfort I used to feel there. But, I am also aware that it still has much to teach me, and I have come to rely on the sound of its bells and whistles whenever I find myself slipping back into old language and habit, whenever I start chanting to myself "I can't."

This experience has made me believe that *any* area of physical stress can be eliminated by letting go of just two things, the need to create it and the fear that it owns you. Just once try calling an illness by its name and asking it: Who's running the show here? Then, look inside and listen to the answer your Higher self provides you.

Try a new approach. Take a stand on healing just one ill in your life. Take a brief vacation from blame. Make one choice in favor of love and forgiveness.

Then look again. See how good the world feels now. See how even your dreams have dared to come closer.

"Swimming Familiar Waters"

Chapter Seven

Swimming Familiar Waters

From the very first time I created a story on paper—a composition about Christmas, which I wrote in the third grade—I wanted to be a writer. As a child, I loved books, but it was never the stories within them that captured my interest. It was the way they were told, the way language could be strung together in limitless combinations of words and images. I had an inborn love of written expression, it seemed, just as some have a gift for music, an eye for color or a bent for mathematic equations. I had an ear which would sort busily through a sentence's syntax and tone while I read, and commit its delicate construction to memory.

From high school, I prepared myself to enter a college writing program, an end which I didn't achieve until the age of 26, for an overriding lack of self-confidence always got in the way of my making a serious commitment to a writing career. There were other career paths I sought temporarily along the way, including one in business and one in teaching, but actually, my heart was never in any alternative to a writing career, and eventually I bored of each diverted path.

In business, I was frequently asked to write or edit letters, proposals and other presentations to company clients. Though it paid me handsomely for doing what I liked—writing—the subject matter never interested me, no matter how practical this avenue seemed, or how nobly I tried to make business my life's work.

When my husband's job transferred us to London in 1986, I took advantage of this opportunity to end the career stalemate I'd been in for many years, and finally find something I *wanted* to do.

From the outset, I kept believing some new career would magically appear; something would just click into place one day. I used to say it would probably turn out to be something that had been sitting right in front of me all along, and when I found it, it would be just what I'd been looking for all along.

That part I was right about. After several years, I at last reclaimed the writing career I had always managed to avoid. But the sense of how easily I would fall into my new career was overly optimistic. My step, though sure of the path it had chosen was hesitant and sometimes faltering. I don't know how to describe it really, but I somehow didn't feel capable of making the commitment that a writing career demanded. Writing—not writing in general, but *my* writing—seemed much too self-indulgent to ever take priority in my life. Others did this, yes, but they always struck me as being so much more creatively gifted.

Even after I had completed two entire books, this one and a novel of some length, my work still seemed incomplete to me, like something that would never really be finished or good enough.

Professionally, I was sitting on the edge of the pool with my feet in the water and calling it swimming. Sometimes I would venture into the shallow end, wading painstakingly out, inch by cool inch into deeper and deeper water. But, I always backed out eventually and returned to the side, once it got too cold around the middle. I wasn't a plunger; I wasn't a diver into deep ends.

When I thought about it, which was rather often, I would say that much of my career ambivalence had to do with the fact that I was born female, although there were certainly some men I knew who shared my syndrome, and some women I knew who did not. At home, it was true I had never been encouraged to achieve *anything*, and nothing I did achieve was ever given any notice. But then again, my brothers had received a similarly lukewarm treatment in the area of *their* career selections.

Despite the fact that my upbringing had provided me with no foundation for this, I had long been aware of the *necessity* of a career in my life, that is, something through which I could express my ideas, something of my own choosing, my own making, a creative side to my life, beyond home and relationship, through which I could do and express and make my mark on the world.

But some emotional inner part was always questioning how likely this really was. There seemed to be something unreasonable almost about the expectation that I could actually do what I wanted for a living and be recognized and paid for it in return.

So, I could not, in clear conscience, blame my gender, or my upbringing, or the other role requirements of my life—like motherhood and marriage—for holding me back from my dream of writing professionally, because underneath, it was my own ambivalence and doubt in my creative worth which disabled me the most.

That was something, it seemed, which had an iron-clad grip on me, something that would always, no matter how strong the impulse and desire, pull me back just as I was about to dive head-first into the deep end of the pool.

***

The Amalfi Coast of Italy, which borders on the Mediterranean, is where my husband and I have vacationed each year of our marriage. The region is astonishingly beautiful, with cliffs that sit high over the sea, and an erratic road that zigzags midway across its great slope of rock. From the very first time we visited, we experienced an incredible sense of peacefulness there, something which I believe is commonly referred to as bliss, and it is for this reason, that we always returned.

One year before I was set to travel there, an astrologer told me this particular part of the world was the seat of my creative energy. I didn't understand at the time what she meant. "There's something that comes out of this place," she had said, "that realigns you with your creative energies."

I imagined at the time this had something to do with the restorative effects our trips to Italy always had on me, but beyond that couldn't really grasp her meaning. I knew too, that I often had strong mystical-type experiences while vacationing there. Messages from my deceased father came frequently into my dreams. Meditations were clear and powerful in content. I would obtain clarity and perspective on the current slant of my life, and my husband and I would always experience a strong sense of renewal in our marriage.

In addition to the soothing affect of the area, and the insight and revelation I experienced while there, I often felt an odd familiarity and comfort in the surroundings. I'm not speaking of the sort of *déjà-vu* sensation people sometimes experience in a foreign country. There was no building or street or actual piece of ground where I had the sense I had stood centuries before. But there was something about the climate, the terrain, the look of the sea from the road above that struck me as so ordinary, there were moments I completely lost sight of the fact that I was even in a foreign country.

Shortly before my husband and I made what was to be our fifth trip to the Amalfi coast, I was nearing the end of my past-life regression therapy with Marion. I had been curious about the roots of my writing profession, and felt I needed to better understand my somewhat ambivalent relationship with it. Were there any particular challenges which a career in writing was meant to afford me? Were there talents I had brought into this life which would be useful to me in my chosen career?

During one afternoon session, I asked myself these questions and, by way of an answer, the following came forth:

J: There are a lot of people around. They have long robes on. One of my brothers and one of my sisters might be there. There seems to be a temple, and a lot of steps with columns. I'm sitting off to the side. I'm a man. My job is to record things and to transcribe speeches.

M: What is your name?

J: Alenon.

M: How old are you?

J: 34.

M: Who do you record things or write speeches for?

J: The state.

M: What country are we in?

J: Maybe Greece. (1-2-3) I'm getting confused because I keep having this sense that this is Atlantis. (1-2-3) I get both Atlantis and Greece.

M: Alright, there may be a reason for that. We'll leave it for now. What else do you see or hear?

J: It's very echoey. People are coming up the stairs and talking. They seem to come here to work out issues. I take down all the proceedings.

M: What kind of issues?

J: Civil issues. Neighbors who don't get along, property settlements, disputes. There's a panel of sages. These people come and state their cases. It's all settled right there.

M: Is this a court?

J: It's like a court, but really more like a forum. It's an open discussion or debate. The people who come are asking for advice; it's not really like a law is made when the sages speak. The people want to go to someone who is an authority and ask for help. So, if they can't settle their disputes, they come to the forum. They discuss the problem openly with the sages and everyone there. The purpose of this forum is to find common ground, not to rule in favor of one person or the other. Both people go away with something. It's almost like an exercise for these sages, a challenge to find the common ground which will be most satisfactory to both parties. It's interesting because people don't come here angry, even though they are having disputes; they know they will go away with something. Because this forum exists, people in this society don't get angry with each other; they just feel that they haven't found the solution to their differences. They go about it like: let's figure this out; let's get the solution. They come here very hopeful and knowing that they're going to find an end to their problems.

M: Tell me about your life, Alenon. Are you married?

J: Yes.

M: Who is your wife?

J: It begins with a C-L. Cliostra.

M: Do you have any children?

J: Yes. Five.

M: What are their names?

J: The oldest is a boy. Something like Leon, short for my name. He might have the same name. There's a boy, then, a girl, then two more girls, then a boy. There's a boy on each end.

M: Can you get the name of the second child?

J: It begins with an O. (1-2-3) Odion.

M: How about the next two girls?

J: Forithia and Dorion.

M: How about the boy?

J: Bothio or something.

M: Are your wife or any of your children in this life?

J: Yes. My brother Don is one of my sons, the oldest I think. I can see the oldest boy and my wife very vividly. I can't really see the others.

M: Is your wife someone from this life?

J: She is my husband.

M: Can you go ahead five years in that life and tell me what's happening?

J: I don't see anything.

M: Alright, go back to the time where you were and go ahead one year.

J: I'm going down some steps. They seem to be very steep; the steps are carved into the hillside. I'm going down to the water.

M: Why?

J: I want to be alone to think.

M: What are you thinking about?

J: There's some kind of change going on.

M: What kind of change?

J: There's a lot of discontent. We don't seem to be able to solve our problems anymore. Things have gotten too complicated.

M: What's happened?

J: There's a split among the wise men, our advisors. They can't agree about some decisions for our future.

M: So, what happens?

J: It seems that some of the people are siding with some of the judges, and other people are siding with other judges. Everyone is very unhappy. Yes, this is *Atlantis.*

M: Go to the next significant part. (Hereafter NSP.)

J: I'm back in the forum. There are people sitting all over the steps. The different wise men or sages get up and speak about what they think we should do. They seem to be so frustrated with one another, that it's very disturbing for us. We feel in some ways that we can't trust what any of them has to offer as a solution, because their egos have gotten in the way.

M: NSP.

J: There's a big storm now. It seems we spent all our time disputing about what we should do, and we didn't do anything. We thought we had more time.

M: So what happens?

J: They calculated it wrong. They knew there was going to be some planetary disturbance of some sort. They knew, but they calculated it wrong.

M: NSP.

J: Some hurricane or something.[11] *Very strong winds. I'm watching my house go down. Everything is going horizontal, trees and everything.*

M: What's happening to your family?

J: They seem to have left the house. I've returned to the house to find them, but they're not there.

M: Do you find them?

J: No, I never find them.

---

[11] Many accounts of the destruction of Atlantis mention volcanic eruption. I saw nothing like this, although I suppose some sort of submarine eruption could have been involved in what Alenon experienced.

M: NSP.

J: I think I've drowned.

M: What makes you think that?

J: I can see the water above me; I can feel it all around me.

M: Before you go on, I want you to go back to the time when you were courting your wife, and tell me what that was like.

J: It was a very formal thing. We were selected to be together.

M: Is that the custom?

J: Yes.

M: Did you love each other?

J: Yes, we got on very well together. We were matched together.

M: Go to the day of your wedding.

J: There's really not a ceremony or anything. We were just sort of selected to be together and we just are. Everybody feels they still have a choice. You do still choose the person; they find you someone, and then you can decide to marry them if that's what you want to do. They pick the person who is karmically and astrologically correct for you. All these things are known. These wise men, these sages have all sorts of psychic powers.

M: So how did it work out?

J: It worked out very well. Everybody here is very happy. Everything works out, and if it doesn't, you take your disputes to the forum. Everybody's free to do what they want to do; nobody has to feel that they're stuck with something, or that they have to do something they don't want to.

M: Did you have any disagreements with your wife?

J: I don't think so.

M: Go to the second year of your marriage. Tell me about the significant part.

J: She's very quiet. She likes staying with the children. She sings and plays music. Sometimes she entertains the people who live here. Whenever you have a talent, you're encouraged to share that talent with others. So there are all these places for people to perform or show the things that they've done, like pottery or paintings, or to share a creative idea. It's all part of the forum, the same concept, in other words, not only do people bring disputes there, but they bring their talents and things they've created and their ideas for the community.
    She likes to do a lot of things with flowers. Sometimes she makes things from flowers. She's very quiet. I don't see her laughing or smiling very much.

M: Can you ask her why she's not smiling much?

J: She says she's not happy.

M: Why?

J: She's always in the background.

M: What do you respond?

J: I feel very surprised. I feel that anything anybody wants to do they can do.

M: Talk to her about it.

J: She says it's harder for her because she's a woman. The men are more easily accepted.[12]

M: What can you do about that?

---

[12] In fairness to Cliostra, I will say that I believe her observations to be correct. In all of the visual images I was able to pick up of this Atlantis, men were very much in the forefront, were very much the decision makers and main actors. The women seemed to play a minor role in the society.

J: She says we're under the illusion that everything is equal. Many things are still expected of you, and so you aren't free to choose.

M: You mean expected of women?

J: No, of everyone. She finds fault with the way we all live, and I don't. I'm very happy, and feel that it's an ideal society. But she feels that people are still sort of pushed in some direction. Even if they don't literally say you have to do this or that, they still sort of expect certain things of you, and so you're not really free if you're doing what's expected of you.

M: Do you try to talk to her about this?

J: We don't talk about this. We're talking about it now, but we never talked about this then. She never said anything.

M: Was she angry inside?

J: More sad and unhappy, disgruntled.

M: In that life did you notice this and try to do something about it?

J: I noticed that she didn't laugh very much, but I thought that was just her personality. She was very quiet and detached, and yet she seemed very calm all the time.

M: If you were in that marriage now, what would you do differently?

J: I wouldn't do anything differently.

M: If you were the wisest person you can imagine, what would you do differently then?

J: I would give her something.

M: What would you give her?

J: Whatever it was that she wanted.

M: Attention?

J: I think she just wanted to be heard.

M: Would you listen to her then?

J: Yes.

M: Go back to the moment of your death and move toward the light and see if there's any wise person there to answer your questions.

J: There's someone there.

M: Is there anything you should have done differently?

J: I should have had more confidence or trust in myself.

M: In what way?

J: I was too much under the spell of the sages. I believed in them too much and didn't exercise my own creative talents.

M: Alright, I want you to think about your questions about writing. What talents did you have in that life that will be helpful to you in this life for your writing?

J: I can see many sides of issues. Not just one or two. There's not just one solution. There's always many.

M: Do you think the experience you had of being a man in that life will be useful to you in this life?

J: Yes. I can understand better how a man thinks.

M: Are there any other strengths that will be helpful to you in your writing?

J: My experiences using creative energy.

M: Ask the wise person if there's anything else you learned in that lifetime that would be useful to you in this lifetime.

J: Just to remember that there's more than one solution or path, that I always think there's just one, but there are many.

M: Can you forgive the people in that life that bothered you?

J: No one bothered me.

M: Can you forgive yourself for your lack of understanding of your wife?

J: Yes.

M: Alright, it's time to come back now.

***

I'd always thought Atlantis to be in the middle of the Atlantic Ocean. When I came home after this session and told my husband about the confusion I experienced at the start of the regression, as I tried to establish myself in either Greece or Atlantis, he said, quite matter-of-factly: "Well, *that's* where it used to be." It amuses me that he knew this, though he claims he doesn't know how he came by this information. The research I later did into this matter revealed that Atlantis *is* believed by some historians to have been situated somewhere in the Mediterranean (south of Amalfi) near the Greek Isle of Crete. (That's my Cliostra for you.)

Others, however, continue to maintain that Atlantis was a large land mass that ran off of the eastern seaboards of North and Central America and extended well into the Atlantic Ocean. Generally, however, Atlantis is thought to be entirely mythical, and to further my research I needed to look through New Age literature, or what I would call alternative sources of historical perspective.

There, I seemed to encounter many negative things about the Atlantians themselves, that they were a people into domination and global control, that they were, in fact, ultimately responsible for their own destruction and a massive altering of the planet Earth, as it had existed then.

I could not reconcile this with what I had taken away from my regression experience. The Atlantian society I remembered seemed devoted to principles of self-actualization, creative expression and peaceful co-existence, not at all like the aggressive and power-hungry Atlantians I read about in my research. Additionally, I had a strong curiosity about what I had referred to during my regression as the sages, and what my relationship with them was like. I also still longed for a clearer connection between my career of scribe in that life and my present-day writing career.

Therefore, I did another regression some years later with a friend of mine, Nancy, in order to shed more light on these areas, and clear up the mystery of Atlantis' location:

N: How did this society originate?

J: We were an offshoot.

N: An offshoot of what?

J: We were a band of people. I was a child when we left, when the society was established. We traveled to this place in boats. From Atlantis. Some of the elders had become disillusioned with Atlantis, and we were allowed to leave.

N: Do you know the name of the place you went to?

J: It's around where Greece is now. We still thought of it as Atlantis.

N: How long before Atlantis was destroyed?

J: Not long.

N: Did the Atlantians know?

J: We knew it was coming. We knew they (i.e, the mother country) would engineer our destruction.

N: How did they do that?

J: It had to do with deflection and intervention of rays, I would say, natural light. They had ways of harnessing solar power, and then they could use it to do different things. They were trying to change our ecosystem, but I think there was also something that had to do with directing solar energy, unprotected solar energy, so that we would be burned out in some way, that's what we thought, at least.

N: Is that why you left?

J: No, they had allowed us to leave. There was a growing group of us who were continually disagreeing with the way things were being run and the direction in which we were headed, and we were tolerated and allowed to leave, although we felt we would ultimately be destroyed. *We were permitted to flourish for a while, and they were basically just waiting to engineer some sort of destruction. Time was very different then. There wasn't the sense of immediacy as there is now. Years and years would pass.*

N: So your society originated from the Atlantians, and you left them because there was this growing dissension and dissimilarity between the two groups, and yet they engineered their own destruction and, ultimately, yours too?

J: Yes.

N: But it was not intentional?

J: No, they were trying to destroy us.

N: And in trying to destroy you, they destroyed themselves?

J: Yes, it was a domino effect sort of thing. There was something they had done to...the original idea was that they would pierce the atmosphere in some way above where we were, they would pierce the natural liner that protected us from the full power of solar rays, and it would cause obviously massive destruction, but they felt that it would be localized. I guess what happened is that there was a domino effect; the destruction of the curtain, caused further destruction, which in turn caused further destruction, and so on. It did not have the effect they thought it would.

N: And did this take a long time to come to fruition?

J: It took a long time to come to fruition, but it did not take a long time to occur. It happened very rapidly.

N: So then, once the process started, did they realize at some point they couldn't stop it?

J: Yes. Yes. They destroyed the curtain, because you couldn't just pierce the curtain. It was like poking a hole in a balloon: the hole doesn't stay; the whole thing goes.

N: What is the relationship between your work in this life, and your work in that life?

J: It has to do with revisiting old ideas. This society that I belonged to was very interested in development of Higher self, self-actualization, operating totally through creative power. It was something I believed very much in, and there is the desire to bring that back, to be instrumental in bringing that back. The world is not the same as it was then, and there has always been this hope that it would return.

N: And what about the relationship between this life and creative expression in general?

J: Well, that life was creative expression; that was what we were devoted to. I'm now learning to regain that devotion. We saw it as an obligation. To us it was the only point in being here. It was a sort of worship, and I think we were criticized for that, but we were in awe of what we were capable of creating. That kind of focus is lost now. Everything was considered creative expression then, even an idea, but we did not worship the individual for the creation, we worshipped and acknowledged the source or power that gave them that capability. We saw it as this source, this energy which each individual would take his own experience into, and he would go into the energy and come out of it holding something, whether it was an idea, or a design for a building, or a painting, or a speech. You would say that I did not write creatively in this life, by current definitions of creative writing, but our definition of creative writing, creative expression, was much different than yours.
The language itself was very complex, probably closer to Chinese than anything that exists today. The symbols were pictorial, conceptual.[13] It was important that we create a written language that would not be limiting, and so each symbol was designed to be somewhat open-ended, like a picture would be. Each person would see something different there and understand it differently, so that the symbol itself wouldn't limit or violate one's own perception. So, proceedings were not taken down word for word, they were taken down in concept. Something that isn't done now. There's nothing like this now. It's hard for me to even explain it. So much of our communication was telepathic; we relied very little on language and tried, in fact, to avoid it. The skill that my work involved was to keep a sense of what had transpired in the proceedings as loose,

---

[13] I later realized Alenon was describing cuneiform, an ancient form of writing which used very angular characters to depict an object or idea. Some believe it to be the most complex and descriptive written language of all time.

and at the same time, as precise, as possible. So, it was not like the work of a court stenographer; it was more like the work of an artist.

We did not worship a God per se, we worshipped a creative source, and everything that we saw around us, including ourselves, was recognized as an outtake, an offshoot, of that source. It meant that we had totally different values than what you see today.

N: How was that attitude different than the other Atlantians?

J: They'd gotten so lost. They had lost their ideals. They focussed only on the power within the energy. They wanted to harness that power and control it for themselves, make it predictable, but that was the very beauty of it, that it was never predictable. The danger is, and what we learned, is that you always must continue to worship the source, not the individual who is an instrument of the source in bringing forth creative expression. That's where the point of confusion was. These men who were creating began to worship themselves as creators, and wanted to own the power for themselves, feeling that they were somehow superior or better owners and users of the power than others. They actually became very uncreative because of it. Nothing seemed to flourish there anymore, and we left, thinking that we could keep these principles alive. These principles were sort of a religion for us. We saw it as a religious difference, rather than a political one.

N: You wanted to know more about the sages. Who were they?

J: Four men, they represented four points of view, as in the four points of the compass, four perspectives. It was thought that they would keep the society open-minded and respectful of all points of view. They assisted in any disputes that were brought before them.

N: So, did they play a role in the law?

J: They didn't make laws per se. The society was very loose (free of form). We basically didn't have laws. And every situation was considered special. Laws were thought to be limiting, because there was always an extenuating circumstance that a law couldn't take into consideration. The society was sort of run that each individual was basically autonomous. However, from time to time there would be conflicts between or among individuals. They would come to the forum and put forth their case, and the sages would present different ways of looking at the situation and suggest ways of resolving the conflict.. There actually wasn't much conflict.

Their perspectives represented the expression of the different concerns of the individual: there was moral—what you call moral—emotional, physical and spiritual. (Moral sort of was like societal obligation). So each would argue from his perspective. They were like priests or gurus, that sort of thing. That was their life's work. And they devoted all their time to it. They had no families or other responsibilities. They were pulling in this energy and they would...you have people doing this now; it's called channelling. That's what you'd call it; we didn't see it that way. This was a skill that they were quite strong in. It was really a much simpler time; things were much simpler then, and yet it's really hard to explain in present-day terms.

N: Why is it hard to explain?

J: Things that were a given for us don't even exist now. You see, the introduction and the enhancement of the destructive element, which of course we always recognized and chose not to develop, is what is ultimately responsible for the polarity of present day. It couldn't be left alone; it had it's attractive qualities, short-sighted, yes, but still attractive. Ultimately, the positive is more powerful because it's longer-sighted, and so in thought it spirals farther out, and that was a given, but at some point the choice was made to enjoy in the short-term all the powers that the positive had in the long-term. That's why destruction seems more powerful to us; it's condensed, but in the long run, it will exhaust itself.

***

Anyone who has ever been engaged in creative or artistic expression of any kind will freely admit that the best, the most inspired and pleasing part of their work comes to them from a part of themselves they can't identify. They will tell you that it doesn't even seem to spring from their own thoughts. It seems to come literally out of nowhere, popping up at the exact moment they stopped *thinking* about what it is they were trying to do. This I believe is the experience which Alenon tried to describe in the above regression, an experience to which his society was devoted, and that is, expressing through the creative consciousness.

The point of confusion that sometimes arises out of this phenomenon (which Alenon elaborates on in his discussion of the original Atlantis) occurs between the creator and the creative source.   From Alenon's viewpoint, the role of the creator (whom we would call artist) is a relatively passive one. Through him comes the inspiration, the revelation, the insight for the creation. He provides only the flavor, because as that inspiration passes through the veil of his individual ego and experience, he will give it his own unique interpretation, but the main ingredient—the inspiration—is not his. He does not own it, he is not responsible for it, nor, in fact, should he take any *personal* credit for it.

The ego's perspective of the creation and its desire to partake in the creative process are of *this* world: what will this get me? What will people think of me because of my having created it? How much money will they give me? How much fame? How much criticism? What will my family say? And, so on. It will argue (as mine often did) that the artist may not have the time or the courage or the skill or the right to take part in the creation. The larger the role the ego plays, the less creative the work will end up. With each overlay of social concern, the glistening jewel, which has been extracted out of the creative consciousness, will be dulled and perhaps obscured all together.

The wise artist, it would seem then, is one who's ego has all but gone to sleep, who knows herself not as a transmitter of creative energy, but as a receiver, through which the creative consciousness dances its wild, spontaneous and perfect dance.

The above regressions did much to drive this home for me, and while I will admit that my rigid, perfection-seeking ego (who is after all, completely incapable of perfection), still gets in the way from time to time and jams up the frequencies with its chatter, I am not so ambivalent anymore about telling it when to sit down and shut-up. As a result, I have found that the deep waters of the pool are not so cold after all, *if* you dive into them head-first.

The experience of this particular past-life recall had many things to teach me. For one thing, I have come to embrace a different and broader definition of the term *creative*. I actually used to view my work as less valuable than other more *practical* professions because it operated out of creative expression. But, the insights rendered through the reworking of Alenon's life showed me that all paths taken in life—all life itself for that matter—are, in some way or other, avenues of creative expression.

More importantly, I learned that each of us has equal creative potential. Those who appear on the surface to be more creative are simply letting down their guard a little more. Creative expression is not something which can be controlled; it is something that must be allowed to pass through us untouched.

Alenon understood this in theory, but did not always embrace it in practice, particularly when it came to his relationship with the society's advisors, whom he called the sages. It is a trap into which we all fall, where we give over our rights to put forth an idea or to try our hand at something new because we believe that others are better at it. We must retrain our thinking in such areas. It is not a matter that someone else's creative contribution is better. It is simply different.

I was not unique to search so hard for my identity in the thing which is my livelihood, hoping it would somehow demonstrate the extent of my self-worth to me and the rest of the world. Like Alenon, I have taken enormous pleasure in recording what I see and hear, what I believe in and understand. But, lately I've become quite certain that writing is not the only arena in which I express myself creatively, and writing alone will never be capable of adequately describing who I am.

Whenever one tries to define himself by a profession or an activity or a talent, he actually stonewalls any potential growth he might experience in that area and severely limits the dimension of who he is. The true sense that we deserve to be here and that our existence has value—no matter what we do—will only come from the recognition that who we are is far broader and more wonderful than career alone can ever hope to tell us.

We all have been many things before, worked at many different jobs, experienced the defeats and successes of many centuries of time, and each single moment of each individual's share in that history has been worthwhile, because it has helped bring us all to the moment in which we now find ourselves. We never have any reason to doubt our worth to society, no matter what we do. Our true value is measured in terms of our potential as humans, which is limitless and constant throughout time.

No path taken, after all is wrong per se, if there is learning to be had in the choosing of it. Yes, I agree there is more of a sense of thrust, or momentum with the paths we choose from the heart, but the bumpy, extraneous roads we travel in getting to them are equally valuable ones.

For that is how I see the history of my career now, not as a series of interruptions or wrong roads mistakenly chosen in preference to the correct one, but as one continuous movement to where I am. I now understand that the occasional intrusion of self-doubt, ambivalence and fear did not impose a threat but an opportunity, an opportunity to confront and wrestle with these emotions for the sole purpose of eliminating them. A necessary course I took in getting to higher, smoother ground. It is no coincidence that as I focussed less on where I was headed and how long it was taking to get there, I felt more creative and enjoyed my work more.

In the end, it *is* nothing more than a shift of focus, an end to our pointless concerns about what mark we will make on the world, in favor of the knowledge that the worth of our existence is a given, and that our mark was carefully inscribed on the face of this planet centuries ago. Past-life regression therapy is one tool that can render us such a perspective, by showing us that though we have already served in many capacities, the importance of each life's work was not measured by what we did, but what we learned while doing it.

* * *

Whether you choose to believe in the existence of the lost civilization of Atlantis or not, the story of Alenon still provides us with an interesting allegory, a sort of parable, in which water could be seen as a metaphor for the creative consciousness. It is the water in which the new Atlantians eventually drowned, because they repeatedly lost sight of the need to listen as well to the requirements of the ego and its fundamental need to endure.

The character of Cliostra gives voice to that ego; she represents the dissenting whisper which Alenon and his colleagues, in their blind devotion to creativity-for-the-sake-of-creativity, failed to hear, so loud and compelling were the rush and motion of the waters in which they swam.

We learn through this story that the ego's concerns, though mundane, must still be valued and recognized as worthy of attention. As deaf as Alenon was to the complaints of his wife, he was also heedless to his own ego and its desire for physical protection against the treachery of mother Atlantis. Through his fate, we see the importance of achieving a liveable balance between the natures of the (worldly) personality and the spontaneous, creative (otherworldly) Higher self. Neither one should really dominate, because on this plane, at least, the relationship between the two is, by necessity, symbiotic.

To me, the tale of Alenon and his Atlantis says, I am not just writer (creator). I am also mother, wife, citizen, friend, and sister, and my aim in reaching a comfort level in my career should not be to arrive at a place where everything else peaceably agrees to become secondary.

Like every true tragedy within the human experience, this story holds within it a valuable learning: that utilizing one's own creative power doesn't just mean taking the deep, unbridled plunge; it also means remembering to come up for air.

"The Light at the End of the Tunnel"

Chapter Eight

The Light at the End of the Tunnel

There was a time when the term "spiritual" might very possibly have been the last characteristic I would have assigned to myself. For a good many years, through my late teens and twenties, I vacillated between agnostic and atheistic schools of thought, with no more than a casual interest in the question of God. What happened to one after death, what made things happen and not happen in the course of life, who judged and determined recompense for rights and wrongs were not issues that kept me awake at night or even, for that matter, idly occupied by day.

I'd been raised in a Catholic family, with both parents devout believers, particularly my father. They accepted all of Catholicism without question, comfortable in the notion that they had been born members of the one, true church of God, and just reward awaited those who followed its doctrines to the letter.

To me, however, it seemed there was a lot to follow, a lot to keep in mind and guard oneself against. We were asked to pay constant attention to our sins and the respective weight of each, there being sometimes so fine a line running between wrong and right, I worried as a child that I might unwittingly overlook something and forget to ask for pardon. The services were long and laborious and steeped in ritual. Just being there made me feel not uplifted, but as if I was doing penance for some dastardly deed.

I suppose the main thing which never sat right with me, though, was the overwhelming emphasis on human culpability, and the wrathful image of God that went along with it, an image the priests and nuns sought to make us so keenly aware of. God, himself—like the Church which taught us about him—was made to seem so arbitrary and distant, so difficult to please. You never knew when you might be offending him in some way with your small mind, your lame and limited humanness. How could you relate to this entity, really, when he seemed so perverse in judgment, so purposefully cruel and fickle, so content to hold back reward from those who were hard-working and devoted?

The fact that there was so much inequity in life had always disturbed me, and the "Lord-works-in-mysterious-ways" kind of shrug which many gave to the matter of this troubling disparity was somehow never enough for me. It explained nothing, and even seemed a bit pathetic in its blind acceptance of one's powerlessness against the capricious twists and turns of life.

At the same time we were being taught of the righteousness of God's displeasure with us, we were repeatedly assured of God's great love and beneficence where we were concerned, how perfect we were in his eyes. I had trouble reconciling these two so-called givens of our Creator, and could not grasp how the two could exist within him simultaneously. I was grappling, yes, with my first introduction to duality—to the paradox of good and evil living side by side. But most troubling for me was the notion that any destructive energy could actually emanate from a Being I needed to believe was *only* good, so good in fact, it would defy any label or definition or sense we might have ever had of goodness.

I could not accept the doctrines of Catholicism as unquestioningly as I observed my parents doing. I have never been able to grab hold of *anything* which didn't make perfect logical sense, and that's why—even before I could articulate the questions that rolled around in my head, as I sat through eight years of parochial school and religious instruction—I never truly adopted Catholicism. Though I received its indoctrination and its sacraments, though I tried to become a follower, none of it ever seemed to sink in, and at the age of seventeen, I gave up the struggle, and the obligation I felt I owed to my parents, and walked away for good.

The belief system I have come to adopt, after being for many years in—to borrow a term—limbo, has no name, really. I would call it an ideology of my own creation, a doctrine put together with whatever felt and sounded right, and seemed true to my inner sense of what life and death were, who or what God was, and what I was supposed to be doing here after all.

Life, it appears to me now, in all its ebb and flow of madness, despair, accomplishment and joy, is quite logical and perfect in form. What's more, it is never, ever arbitrary. *Everything* happens for a reason, and when it does, it happens exactly as it was intended to. Even the unfortunate parts.

It's hard to accept this, even harder to accept that we are in some ways responsible for it. But the fact is, negative experience arises out of negative thought, and that negative thought comes from us, not from God.

Might we then go so far as to say if God didn't create it, then it cannot exist? Is negative experience then nothing more than illusion? Well, let's consider an example. A young person dies unexpectedly. To those who loved her, this is a horrible tragedy. Someone dear is lost to them, her life is ended prematurely, their own lives are irreparably shattered. Is *this* an illusion?

Higher self would say this: the young woman is not lost, she is right here, she never went anywhere. The young woman is completely safe, always was and always will be. Her life is not over, because her soul is immortal. The experience through which her soul was expressing itself has changed, nothing more. It is not her survivors' love for her that makes them feel their sorrow; it is their unawareness that the girl has not been taken, and their inability to communicate with her on this new plane of experience she has entered. If they were certain of her continued presence, how could their lives be shattered?

I do not mean to trivialize in any way the experience of having a loved one die or the sorrow that comes out of that experience. It has happened to me, and I, too, have been devastated by it. What I'm trying to say is that embracing the principle of eternal life of the soul will automatically beg these questions. You can't accept mortality, if you truly embrace *im*mortality. You're either one or the other. You can't be both.

It all comes down to a matter of perspective. In this plane of experience that we call life on Earth, we tend towards a dualistic perspective. We see in our reality poverty and wealth, sickness and health, beauty and ugliness, love and loneliness, life and death, and so on and so on. Does the duality really exist, or is it just our perception?

Let me intercede with a little analogy here. You go to a movie and are given a pair of 3-D glasses to wear for the viewing. During a fight scene in the film, one of the characters lunges at the screen with a knife. The glasses make it seem like the actor is actually coming toward you, and you instinctively jump back in fright. Now then, does this experience mean that the actor really did lunge out of the film at you? Are you damaged in any way? If you hadn't been wearing the glasses, would you have even responded the same?

Duality strikes me as a perspective that operates much the same in our Earth experience. Actors only *seem* capable of harming you in this 3-D world, but that is a mirage. In truth, they can do nothing to harm you.

It is when you come to believe the duality, believe that the 3-D world *is* the reality that your expectations and understanding and attitudes completely change. If you believe that you are a helpless creature, that people are evil and are out to harm you, that life is unbearable, that wealth and your access to it are limited, that death and disease are a heartbeat away, then your experience will reflect those thoughts. If you believe instead that the universe is infinitely abundant and will always provide for you, that you are a powerful entity who has chosen to be here, that you are safe and well-protected, that death will only come if you choose it, then your experience will reflect *that*. Beauty and ugliness both exist because in our world we have both beautiful and ugly thoughts.

It seems to me when I look at the image of the wrathful God, that *that* God is one created in the image of man, and not the other way around. It is we humans, steeped so much in duality that we have come to call it truth, who are responsible for keeping the pot of gold away from our own eager hands. Why would God, who is perfect, and who created us in that image ever regard us as flawed or undeserving of anything?

If we look for a moment at the Earth, in its pure and undamaged state, we can understand more fully the magnificent perfection of which God is capable. The Earth, disregarding for a moment the careless violation it has endured from humans, is truly a Garden of Eden, completely self-sustaining and ever-abundant, never lacking in beauty or diversity. Even now, with so much pollution and waste and assault from its human inhabitants, it is still beautiful, still capable of healing itself, and still so powerful and elegant in form that it brings tears to the eyes of anyone who has the rare privilege of viewing it from outer space.

Like all universal matter, the Earth is completely capable of correcting its own imbalances—the sort of phenomena which we prefer to call acts of God. In the history of its own terrible power—manifestations like floods and earthquakes and fire—has actually come thicker and more lush vegetation, new species of animals, more temperate climates, restructured and exotic terrain.

The Earth is, in a way, a wonderful enlarged version of ourselves, as we, too, are perfect creations of God. We also have the power of creating our own balance within the world in which we exist. Our choices are limitless and infinite—our gift of free will from a Creator who loves us. Thus we may bring about our own quakes and fires, in the form of loss or physical pain or destruction of the things we value, with the higher purpose of clearing away the emotional debris that weighs us down, setting right the priorities we have misplaced, and arriving at a new space of clarity and lightness. This, after all, is the process of life—a learning process—our only point of existence, our sole purpose in coming to Earth. What we resist learning will linger for all eternity; what we embrace and confront and break through will trouble us no more, and leave instead something beautiful and new in its wake.

The home which God provided us is a powerful teacher. We are inextricably bound to it, because it is a keen reflection of who we are and the roots from which we come. What we put into it, it gives back in kind. We nurture it, and it yields great things to feed and protect us; we destroy it with pollution, and it yields carcinogens that in turn endanger us.

And like humans, when threatened with destruction, the Earth finds other ways to survive. The valuable lesson humankind will learn from the great task of restoring the Earth to its original state of health—the enormous and pressing challenge it now faces—is that, being perfect creations, we have the power to both accomplish this task, and the choice to undertake the repair or continue the destruction.

It is the same choice we face at every moment of our own lives. Do we continue to indulge the unhealthy and addictive behaviors of our personalities, or do we replace the destructive patterns, which bring only unhappiness and loss, with self-sustaining and nurturing ones? This after all is what is meant by free will; it is a universal law which says to us: in this world (the world of good and evil) you will always have a choice. Choose the positive thought or action and your experience will be full of lightness; choose the negative, and your experience will be full of sorrow. You choose. Whatever you select will be given.

The difference between these two prerogatives is sometimes hard for us to even discern. But each has a very different impact or effect on our lives and the lives of others. What that means is simply this: the realized benefit from negative action is short-lived, from positive, long-lived.

For example, it is perhaps both cost-effective and convenient for a manufacturer to dump hazardous waste into the stream which runs by its factories, i.e., beneficial in the short-term. In the same way, it is possibly fun and relaxing to sit with friends and get drunk night after night. But in the long term, neither of these actions results in any true measure of *benefit*. In fact, both will prove ultimately detrimental to life, health, and the potential for future happiness.

When we ponder the source of our own misery, we need look no further than to our own malevolent power. The individual, who by following the expedient whims of his ego, pollutes the stream and ignores his friend, strikes his child and lies to his boss is the same person who is responsible for the loneliness, sorrow and pain within his heart, for the frustration of his goals and dreams, and for the aches and suffering of his own body. There is no rationale for pinning the blame on the loving Being who created you. Pain, suffering and negativity beget pain, suffering and negativity. Because our Creator does not know such things, it has no motive or resource with which to create them.

Within our human experience, fortune—good and bad—is as varied as people are themselves. Everyone comes from a completely unique past, to which they have responded in completely unique ways. We see bad things happening to people who do not seem to deserve misfortune, and the inequity seems profound, but all of us are capable of faulty thinking. All of us are capable of believing we are inherently flawed; we are all capable of demonstrating hatred, resentment, anger and fear towards ourselves and others. So, just as there must always be an egg before there is a chicken, any life event, good or bad, must be preceded by a respective positive or negative thought from which it grows.

***

Past-life regression therapy, in its process, offers a window into the broader reaches of our universe. We tend to become very myopic in our incarnate form, defining "world" as only the finite space of our earth. Though the field of science and the exploration of outer space have brought us more understanding of the solar systems which surround us, again, we tend only to focus on the physical matter of stars, suns, planets and moons, and not on the infinity which envelops them. Many of us tend towards even more parochial perspectives, seeing only country, community, or even family as our "whole world".

Generally speaking, we have no trust or faith in the non-physical or unseen. If we can't see it, it doesn't exist. And so we discount the entire spiritual world, of which our little Earth is a very tiny, though not insignificant part. What glimpses we are allowed into this other world, we quickly discredit as "only our imagination" or, worse, a hoax. We have been given access to this part of our world not only through past-life recall, but also through channeling, psychic phenomena, out-of-body experiences, near-death experiences, dreams, communications with the dead, angel sightings, miraculous healing and even the odd, and completely inexplicable "coincidence". And generally, we trust none of it. Even when we have no other explanation for these occurrences, we still will not give their existence and their "realness" the benefit of the doubt.

To me, one of the biggest obstacles we face as humans is how caught up we are on the *physical*. Consider, for instance, a very strange practice which has come out of the science of cryogenics—people who have their bodies frozen after they die, in order that they may be "reawakened" when a cure is found for the condition which killed them. This is severely limited thinking. The real person is the energy or spirit form inside the body, not the physical space which houses it. The body is merely a temporary vehicle or shell through which the spirit expresses itself in one particular fashion or another. Once that particular expression—or life—has been completed, the spirit moves on to a new challenge, new learning, and, if desired, a new physical body and incarnation. If there were any purpose for the spirit to continue life in the body which is now being stored in a freezer somewhere in California, it would not have left that body in the first place.

While we are on earth, the area which requires greater focus than the physical space which embodies us is the realm of the *emotions*, with which we express and experience thought. Everything which is physical is actually wrought from emotional expression. Everything we have ever created, we have created from need—the need for attention, comfort, protection, happiness, or pleasure. What motivates us to do anything from writing a letter, to inventing the computer chip is the desire to do it. With intellect alone, we would not be moved to build skyscrapers or search for the cure for cancer. While we have the pure intellect to do most anything imaginable, we will not undertake something as our life's work unless we have the emotional commitment or motivation to do so. Some emotional component is the necessary impetus for *all* of our accomplishments as humankind, and a greater comprehension of our emotional depth and nature as human beings is one of the primary reasons we manifest our spirit forms on this plane. Emotion is the energy that manifests thought into reality.

Emotions are also the driving force behind our *karma*. Without guilt, we would not feel compelled to punish ourselves; without self-doubt, we would not feel compelled to test ourselves; without love, we would not feel a sense of duty, or attraction to other souls; we would not remember our bonds or the obligations inherent in them.

Interestingly enough, emotions, though unseen, are perhaps, the only non-physical forces of which we fail to doubt the existence. We cannot taste, smell, hear, touch or see love, but none of us would doubt either its existence or its power, anymore than we would deny the existence of hate, jealousy, anger, unhappiness or fear. We know that they exist because we "feel" them, just as we may "feel" there is someone in the room with us, though we can see no one, just as we may "feel" we are being asked to do something, though nothing has been spoken, just as we may "feel" that everything will turn out alright, though tangible evidence would have us believe otherwise.

Before we came to this earth, we created a physical design for ourselves (and the existence we are living) out of the emotional baggage we carry from other lives. It is a phenomenon to which Yoga masters refer as *samskara*, or a sort of soul memory of prior acts.

Emotional debris from this and other lives is heavily layered like silt in the bottom of a river. These layers tell the story and represent the residue of centuries of events: the passing of many seasons, life forms which have come and gone, periods of drought and periods of deluge. True self lies somewhere underneath all these layers.

And so it becomes quite difficult for us to see pure reality, the reality of our power and perfection, our godliness and our higher destiny. The distortion which gets in the way and makes us see things differently, what motivates us to create other realities for ourselves—like loneliness and pain and sorrow—is the veil of emotional debris we are forever striving to unload. It seems the more we struggle to work through the layers, the more layers we pile on, the more checkered the pattern becomes, and the more we gravitate toward the people who will hurt us, the parents who will tyrannize us, the lovers who will break our hearts.

The Greek myth of Sisyphus, the greedy king forever doomed to push a huge rock uphill, only to see it fall back down again, is a true reflection of the human condition. Each time we feel we've reached the summit and gotten clear of one particular burden, we realize another challenge is just beginning. Sometimes it hardly seems worth it to carry on the struggle.

Even when the first rays of enlightenment start breaking over the confusion of our lives, our natural tendency is to slump back again into doubt and despair. After all, progression of the soul is not a straight line, but a sort of spiral: we progress a little, we back track; we progress a little, we back track. We travel many roads over and over again before leaving them behind for good.

When I first entered past-life regression therapy, I was overwhelmed by the changes it effected in my daily life. I experienced a great sense of spiritual awakening and revelation; I was learning not only about my individual experience, but it seemed of the human experience in general. I felt at last I was really breaking through into an awareness for which I seemed to have been waiting for centuries. The effect was exhilarating, the sense of relief almost palpable.

Then, it seemed, almost without *reason*, my perspective changed. It was as if I had reached the summit and the rock I was pushing had suddenly spilled away downhill. In that moment it felt as if I had gone nowhere at all, that the progress had been an illusion, and nothing in my life had really changed at all.

It didn't seem that answers were even enough, because the world around me was really no different and I still had to operate in it, still had to struggle just the same as before. My loved ones would still do things to hurt and disappoint me; I would still get angry and lose my temper, slam my bedroom door and beat the bed on occasion. So, what was the point?

One day, during therapy, I was articulating all of my disillusionment to Marion. Her suggestion was to use the session that day to provide new hope or clarity for me by going on a search through my memory for a life experience which had been positive and inspirational. Just as our present life is full of negative and positive forces and events, so too are our other lives. Just as we might lift our spirits by counting our blessings now, we can also browse through the archives to uncover far more blessings which have come our way through time.

The session which came out of the directive which Marion gave me that day was the most remarkable of all, and this is what I learned:

J: I'm getting someone in a white robe and sandals, a man. Also, a Roman gladiator.

M: Are they in the same life?

J: Yes. I see the man in the white robe standing, facing me. The Roman soldier is turned to the side. It's a street or marketplace. I'm standing in a crowd. The man in the robe is approaching me. He has a wonderful presence around him. It makes you feel very peaceful to be around him. I think this is Jesus. I'm standing in the crowd. He's walking around touching people's hands. I'm following him down a street. It's amazing. He exudes peaceful power. I feel like I want to be around him forever.

He's stopping on a hillside and people are sitting down. He's waiting for people to gather so he can talk. My brother Bracken is there. His name is Saul.

M: What's your name?

J: Esther.

M: How old are you, Esther?

J: About 20.

M: Are you Jewish?

J: Yes.

N: How did you first encounter Christ?[14]

---

[14] There are sections of this regression which were guided years later by my friend Nancy Grasso. Her questions and my answers are interspersed throughout the original transcript guided by Marion. All Nancy's questions are designated by an underscored letter N.

J: First I heard about him. He was travelling our way. There was a man who was a carter, that's what he did, carted things back and forth, and he came and told us. We didn't believe him. We didn't believe any of it. He talked about the miracles. Well, I mean, it's like anything. So much of it was exaggerated or altered or fabricated, but in the beginning we thought it was all fabrication.

He came into town, Jerusalem, and there were hordes of people with him. He always had hordes of people with him. He was able to attend to them all, able to address their fears even if they couldn't articulate them. I found him to be much more spectacular than anything that had been said about him. Stories about him have always diminished him. He wasn't like anything or anyone we had ever seen, and it was clear that he had a quality about him that wasn't human. He gave off a sort of glow, and I remember shaking hands with him and looking at his hands to try to figure out what he was made of, because he really didn't look like he was flesh. I mean, he was and he wasn't, and when I shook hands with him, I was squeezing on his hand to see if he was actually solid, because he didn't look like he was. People were always touching him, just to see if he was real; he thought it was very amusing and he never minded it. It seemed like when he walked through town, he dragged a whole cloak of people after him. You could just never get enough of him.

M: What's happening?

J: Jesus has gotten up to talk. I feel overwhelmed by him. He's talking and he has an amazing presence. I can't hear him.

M: Move closer.

J: He says, "Everyone is unique in the eyes of God and yet the same. We are all part of God, everyone. God will give us everything we need to be what we're meant to be. This is promised. You don't have to worry. Everything you need will come to you in its time. These things are written and promised. I can tell many stories to make each of you see how God loves you. Each of you has a story. What you see now is only a small part of what there is. God sent me here to tell you this."

There are people asking him questions. A man says, "Why is there so much pain and suffering?" He says, "Only that you can learn. You must learn all these truths, that we are one and God is in us."

There is a woman who says her daughter is very ill and in so much pain, she can't believe she's learning anything but pain. He says, "Even now your daughter knows more than you do. The more there is pain, the quicker we learn."

I say to him, "Why does there have to be pain for us to learn?" "It is written this is how we will learn, because we have lost the way. We have all lost the way. We are God's lost children and that is why we are here."

He says, "We need pain to show us the way. It's like a man who teaches his horse how to get to the market and back. He does it by tugging on the reins. The pain we feel is like the bit in the mouth of the horse, always being pulled, always being tested. We have issues that become really sore for us (like the horse's mouth), but when we break through, there will be no pain after that, and that is how it will be on all issues until it is done."

M: Go on to the next significant part. (Hereafter NSP.)

J: He says (to me): "You don't realize what you can teach yourself. You have knowledge from many centuries. That knowledge is there for the asking. Everything I've told you, you've already forgotten. Now you must learn again, until you remember forever. Why do you test yourself repeatedly? You have no reason to question yourself, because you are perfect in the eyes of God. Your questions come from a dark place inside yourself, which must be healed. Only you can heal it.

"Not because of anything that you do, but because of who you are. You have the power to heal yourself. You have everything you need. You must never feel alone or afraid."

M: NSP.

J: There's a crowd and there's a man who's very deformed, shrunken. One shoulder goes up high. Jesus goes over and puts his thumbs on the man's forehead and his hands around the man's head. The man's body straightens out, although he still looks very pale and thin. The man weeps and weeps. He keeps holding onto Christ's robe, and Christ says, "Go on; you're okay now."

Jesus starts making jokes. He's laughing and the crowd is laughing. He glows; his aura is amazing. Who could kill this man? He glows.

There's a lot of pushing in the crowd. Everyone is very happy. It's like a celebration to follow him through the streets. He loves children; he carries a lot of them, they hang onto his robes. They're drawn to him. They can see his magnetism, and they cling to him.

M: NSP.

J: It's nighttime. There's a fire going. There's a rumor that Christ has been captured. My brother and I have been celebrating Passover. We came out into the square because we heard Christ had been taken. No one seems to know what's going on.

M: NSP.

J: We're standing on a hill, my brother and I. We're looking at the crosses over on the next rise. My brother won't let me go over, because I'm too emotional. I want to get closer. It seems like the end of the world. I don't understand how they could kill this man. Even if they couldn't understand him, all they had to do was look at him. I don't know what we'll do now. My brother says, "He only came to bring the message. He wasn't meant to stay. He was trying to teach us what he meant about pain—that you have to experience pain to find your way back to the Father."

M: NSP.

J: I'm in my house. My brother's trying to get me to eat something. He seems to understand better what has happened. The Jews who followed him didn't condemn him to death. They tricked us.

M: What do you mean by that?

J: It was Passover. There was no one around, so they came and took him. They couldn't get near him any other time. There were too many people around him. They say we turned him over, but we weren't even there. We think they must have paid the street people, the beggars to pretend they were Christ's followers and condemn him. The Romans were afraid of his power, so they took him. They were afraid they would lose control. He was too big.

M: NSP.

J: It's nighttime. I'm lying in bed. I can't sleep. I'm so upset by this. I can't believe this has happened.

M: NSP.

J: Someone comes. I'm running. The tomb is empty and everyone is running. Everyone thinks the body has been stolen. Everything is chaotic. People wonder if the Romans took it. We go home. That's what we think; that they were afraid of a riot. They say we did it, just like they say we turned him over to them.

M: NSP.

J: The word is out that he's been seen. We don't know what to make of it. We think perhaps because he was so powerful, that he could heal himself. We don't know what to believe. There are so many rumors.

M: NSP.

J: I'm at a table with my brother and we're talking. We don't know what to make of all this.

M: NSP.

J: I keep seeing his image everywhere. I keep thinking I see him. I feel I'm so upset, I don't know what I'm doing anymore.

M: NSP.

J: There are some people up on a hill. We've come to talk about what's going on. Everyone admits to having seen him. We're just mystified. We don't know.

M: I'll count to three and then you'll be sure. (1-2-3.)

J: He appeared to everyone.

M: To you?

J: Yes, to everyone who loved him.

N: Looking back on this experience now, ask yourself what was the main thrust of his teaching?

J: Well, he was the teaching. I mean, that was it. I would say that he was the light at the end of the tunnel, he was like, this is it, this is what you're shooting for. I mean, enough said. He was something out of time,

I think. He was like a time traveller. We would say what is this guy doing here, there was very much a sense of that when you were around him, it was like where did he come from? He was clearly out of something that we were completely unfamiliar with, and yet you knew you belonged with him at the same time.

Well, I think he was meant to keep us from despair and ultimate self-destruction, because if there's not an indication that there's something profoundly better, then what's the point? So, here was this possibility that could be sort of pressed and preserved in memory, so we could survive. We were lucky to have the glimpse, but it was meant to be brief.

I think the other thing that was important, and again it was not so much what he taught but the way he was, was (how) he demonstrated the lack of separateness between us and everything else. There was no else with him. When he walked, it almost seemed like all the people who walked with him were kind of glued together, and it was not just visually, it was emotional, automatic, not something you worked at maintaining, just how you felt. Your life and all of the things that you were concerned about were instantly unimportant, and without him saying anything at all, you were able to understand that the Oneness was it, that was what it was all about, and that the laundry or where you were getting your next meal was completely unimportant.

<u>*N*</u>*: How were these things forgotten?*

J: Well, it was the duality. They were forgotten almost immediately. When he was killed, it was as if everything swung back, even further than it had been; that everything had been lost, that there was no meaning in anything. It was hard for us to remember because we don't see the Oneness. We may remember it with our hearts but not our eyes. The eyes are temporal; we see what's around us and think that's how it is. But in our hearts it's not forgotten; it's there that we understand what's good and what's not. And we can always find his love there. It's not forgotten. We just think it is.

<u>*N*</u>*: What happened to you and your brother after Christ died?*

J: My brother became a preacher of sorts, and I travelled with him. Many people did this. We are told of the twelve disciples, but there were many, many disciples at that time. I probably would have given up if it hadn't been for my brother. He felt that the whole point of Christ's dying was for us to carry this information out, to keep alive this way of being. So, that's what we did. We modeled our lives after Christ. People fed us.

We went here and there. Slept where we could. My brother was a good speaker, very inspiring and intelligent. He seemed to understand the big picture more than I could. We had a nice life.

<u>*N*</u>*: How did you die?*

J: Well, I have to admit that part of me never recovered from the death of Christ, and I fought a long battle with despair. There were times when I didn't see the point of going on. I never was able to understand in any sense how anyone could have actually put him to death because he was so indisputably good in every sense of the word. It made me despair about humanity, life and the work my brother and I were doing. If it hadn't been for my brother, I would surely have gone mad. But I did have this conflict always. Basically I died because I wanted to. After awhile I got very tired, dispirited and ill—a cough of some sort. I was quite happy to die, to end the conflict, I would say. I mean if He couldn't move these people, I would think, how could we? But I was always inspired by my brother. He kept me alive to the end.

M: Ask Christ what is the reason for your despair?

J: He says there is no reason for despair. That I shouldn't feel despair because of what happened to him, or because of anything that happens. Not ever. There is nothing to despair about. Despair is illusion; despair is forgetting who you are.

M: Ask him for his blessing, and come back when you're ready.

***

The thing which has always struck me as quite odd about the process of past-life regression is that rather than opening up my sense of existence into a wide gaping space that spans centuries of experience, it has in the end, tended to make my perspective of time seem denser and more compact, like a line which becomes bolder and bolder-faced, by the retracing of a pen. Because of their accessibility, the outer reaches of recorded history have lost their former mystery and foreignness; exotic cultures and ancient periods of time have become ordinary and commonplace.

What strikes me most, and particularly after having experienced the regression recorded above, is how repetitive, i.e., karmic, life is. Something in the phrase: "everything I told you, you've already forgotten, and now you must learn again until you remember forever," for me, completely sums up the human condition throughout history. Here we are, going round and round in circles, lifetime after lifetime, replicating our misery, like some needle stuck in a groove.

On the face of it, the cure seems quite simple. We need to change our negative thought patterns. We need to stop questioning. Stop worrying. Stop trying to control everything. Stop doubting our inner glory. *We need to let go.*

It's like someone taking you to the top of a cliff and telling you that you've always been able to fly. Would you take the leap? In the same manner, we are weighted down in everyday life by the supposed *gravity* of our daily responsibilities: getting our children fed, getting to work on time, getting an education, getting a book written, getting the car fixed, and so on. We forever have the illusion that we cannot operate, that we cannot keep all the balls in the air if we lose control, if we "let go".

But letting go, doesn't mean the elimination of all that we're doing, but *how* we go about doing it. It means the elimination of self-doubt, for instance, or the energy we waste during the actual writing of the book, wondering if we're doing the right thing or if we can actually finish it. It means the elimination of a sense of limitation or lack, i.e., how am I going to pay for the car to be repaired? It means letting go of the morbidity and pessimism which makes us provoke ourselves with an endless barrage of what-if scenarios: what if I lose my job? What if I get cancer? What if my husband dies? What if our house burns down?

Just as we have lost touch with our original awareness of our greatness and perfection as beings, we have lost touch with the original message brought to us by Christ. What Jesus went to the trouble of coming here to tell us was that there is always hope, even when we feel nothing but despair; that where we see failure, there is the success of a lesson learned; that what we see as all-encompassing and all-important, is really just a small part of what there is. We have more power and more knowledge than we could ever need to do what we need to do here, and if we fail to accomplish what we set out to do, we will be given an infinite number of opportunities to try again.

But what happened to the message of hope and comfort that was brought at great expense to the soul who is Jesus? It was passed through the filter of human emotion and limited perception—the veil of duality—adapted to existing cultures and super-structures and transformed in ways which made it more useful to the powers-that-be. Just as Christ was killed because his power was feared by those "in control," the power of his teachings—intended for our advancement—has likewise been defused. Historically, Christian teaching has been used for political purposes and has worked arm-in-arm with imperialism, oppression and paternalism. As the world was Christianized, so, too, was it brought under the control of the reigning power structure, be it Roman, Byzantine, Spanish, British, French or American. And with that Christianization came the message of "accountability," with which we are so familiar, i.e., if you're bad, this big powerful Being up in the sky, who sees all and knows all will punish you for it.

Jesus' message of power and hope and forgiveness wouldn't work well to quell and tame the masses, so one was created which did. Even now I believe that a great deal of what we read as Christ's teachings are abridged and adapted versions of the real thing.

I find it disheartening that these teachings, intended to enlighten, uplift and free us, have repeatedly been used to perpetuate and justify exclusionism, misogynism, racism, and massive condemnation of the human spirit. As humans, we all hold ourselves too accountable already, and the purpose of any organized church or place of worship should be to provide spiritual salving and reassurance of our godliness and inner glory, not to exacerbate the tendency toward self-loathing and judgment to which we already lean.

Unfortunately, the preoccupation of many religious institutions has too often been with the commission of sin, rather than with the advancement of our spiritual awareness. And we have gotten snagged on this negative focus, keeping mental score cards of our own falterings as well as those of others, laying judgment and blame as required, recommending appropriate punishment, and in some cases, insuring that it is rendered.

The commonly imposed belief that God is a being external to us, with a nature and power completely distinct from our own nature as humans, is in a large sense the reason we so blindly accept our own wretchedness. We are miserable and erring and flawed because we believe that that is, has always been and will forever be, our true nature.

It is reasonable to assume that this entangled web known as life on the planet Earth began sometime or other, and whether we are in a state of progressing forward from the Neanderthals we once were or whether we are in a state of trying to recapture the superhumanness of say, the Atlantians, is not really important. What is important is *why* we are here.

It would seem that, as creations or offspring of a super Being or Creator, we desired at some point, as we continue to desire at the start of each lifetime, to experience our creative power on a plane which would make us *seem* individualized; to learn, to teach and to question, rather than to know; to make and build and experiment, rather than to witness what has already been accomplished. Because we asked for such an opportunity, we were given free will, or a will separate from our

Creator's, with which to do this. On the down side, we were also given the ability to feel pain—emotional and physical—as a sort of built-in checks and balances system. Pain is really no more than a flag or an alarm which sounds in a particular area of the emotions or the body—or the world for that matter—to let us know we need to pay attention to some imbalance or inequity.

If we were ever to take advantage of our godly powers by harming ourselves or others, the alarm would go off. It's safe to assume that some one of us was guilty of beginning this unfortunate trend somewhere along the line and perhaps that is where the notion of original sin was born.

But that trend does not discount the fact that by nature we are not sinners; we are not evil and we are not wretched, lowly beings. It does not even imply the necessity of judgment or punishment, because the universe itself is capable of correcting all its imbalances. It is safe to say that in this world we have become obsessed with our own wrongdoing, and we have forgotten completely or chosen to ignore the fact that we are in reality powerful, loving, superior beings created in the image of God.

***

An essential component of the teaching of Christ is that eternal life and splendor *are* obtainable on Earth, even while engaged in the experience of the human body.   But, his uniqueness and the miraculousness of his existence rest with the fact that he successfully accomplished this feat, *not* that he was capable of it.

Why then, we might well wonder, did he die such a macabre and hideous death? Surely it was not an experience produced out of his own sense of fear and disillusionment, because he simply would not have entertained such emotions. Nor was the death something he couldn't have protected himself against had he desired to do so. The only explanation that can reasonably be given here is that he volunteered for it; he agreed to it in order to enact the *true* drama of the human experience.

His death and subsequent resurrection, his bodily assumption into heaven, are all pure metaphor. He did it to show it could be done! It is what is meant by the phrase: He died for our sins. He died and came back to life as demonstration and proof of our immortality, because we were misguided enough to actually believe that our story—and his—ended with death.

Christ did not have his own karma; he had achieved a perfect state of grace. He was not engaged in the experience of torture and death for his own learning or evolvement.   He was already evolved.   It was an experience he engaged in *for us* to dramatically show just how invincible the physical body is when it is completely aligned with the spirit entity within, an entity which cannot contemplate the limitations which death imposes.

On some level I believe we all still hold the purity of Christ's message within us, no matter how distorted the form in which it has sometimes been rendered. I am certain that no matter how lost we have been, how much we have forgotten about ourselves, we continue to receive valuable hints of our own inner glory.

All is by no means lost. We could say, in fact, that nothing is lost, because this universe is one of infinite abundance, and Earth is not the only creative opportunity that we will be given in our eternal lives.

In the meantime, we have our memories of promise, occasional glimpses—like Jesus Christ—into our true splendor, and numerous gifts with which to attain that splendor. To that end, we come to realize, even despair is a gift, because it reminds us how far away we have fallen. It feeds our desire for something better and provides the miracle that makes us arise and begin the long climb back home.

Appendix

Regression Exercises

I am including in this section two sample meditations which can be used to acquire past-life information. The first past-life regression meditation was originally designed for a group seminar on the subject. It is aimed at giving someone, who is a complete novice, a taste of what regression feels like, but it is not recommended as a tool for actual therapy sessions. The text is intentionally fanciful in order to raise the comfort level of the subject going into the regression, and therefore provides a visual experience that is more relaxing than it is therapeutic.

The second exercise is more lengthy and involved, but, again, is not structured to evoke an actual regression therapy session. Though still somewhat exploratory in nature, this exercise is best guided by someone who is skilled in the process. It would not be particularly fruitful or easy to attempt on your own.

It's important to reiterate that past-life regression is a powerful form of therapy and should be approached sensibly, with the help and guidance of a professional.

Past-Life Regression Exercise I

Lie down and get comfortable. Take a few deep breaths, long and slow, each one longer and deeper than the last. (PAUSE.)

Allow your mind to wander freely, allow it to go off in a direction of its own choosing. Let go of the need to control your thoughts. Let your mind just babble. (PAUSE.)

Allow your mind to wander until it comes to settle on a particular issue or problem of its own choosing. Something it spends a good deal of time on. Remove yourself from the problem and watch your mind work it through, as if you were listening to a close friend tell you about his problem.

As you listen to the problem, try to identify some of the emotions present in this situation. See each of them as a separate, tiny stone, and examine each one of them in your hand, as you take inventory. Perhaps you pick up a spiky, brittle stone of jealousy? A sharp, sticky pebble of anger? A cold, hard stone of hatred? A tarry, black chip of fear? (PAUSE.)

Hold all of the stones in the palm of your hand and look at them very carefully. Then cup your hands and close them around the stones until you can no longer see them. Rattle the stones around inside your cupped hands. This sound is the sound that keeps you awake at night. It's the sound of your despair.

Hold your hands still now, and imagine yourself pressing all these stones together. Realize that as you press on them, they begin to break down and mash together like clay. Push all the hard, sharp stones into one tight, small clay bundle. (PAUSE.)

Choose now to deny this little bundle the property of gravity. In other words, find that you need to hold onto it now or it will float away from you like a helium balloon.

When you feel comfortable doing so, let the bundle go. Watch it float skyward until it is the size of a pinpoint, and then, watch it disappear completely from your sight.

This exercise has enacted for you a power that you already own, the power to take away—in the wink of an eye—your own pain and confusion.

***

Now, I want you to imagine that you are a cell floating through space, slowly descending to earth. Sense yourself descending through layers of stratosphere, through blue sky and clouds, down until you see a land or seascape. Perhaps you see a town or city, filled with rooftops. Let yourself wander freely over this space. Observe it as you float by, and when you feel inclined to land, begin to do so. Realize you have the ability to push through any rooftop into any enclosed space, if you desire, or you may choose to land on the ground or on a mountain or a boat. Land anywhere you wish. (PAUSE.)

As a cell, you have no particular attachment to anything on this planet. You are merely here to observe. You are here to experience. Investigate what's going on around you. (PAUSE.)

What is the weather like? It it cold, hot, rainy, sunny? Is it nighttime? Are there people nearby? Can you hear them talking? What are they saying? What smells are around you? What is this space like? Experience what it is to just exist without obligation, or struggle. You have absolutely no attachment to anything in this life. You just are. Experience your surroundings. Observe the life around you. (PAUSE.)

I want you to now realize, again without any particular concern, that as a cell, you have become part of the matter that makes up some particular person. Who is that person? What do you sense about them? Are they male or female? Young or old? Wealthy or poor? Hardworking or lazy? What are the things which concern them? What emotional attachments do they have? What is their family life like? (PAUSE.)

If you can, ask them what their name is. Ask them where they live. What year it is. Ask them if they have anything they would like to share with you, anything they would like you to know. An experience, a piece of advice, a thought. (PAUSE.)

Realize now that you have complete knowledge and understanding of this person, and that you feel nothing but love and compassion for them. Thank them for having contributed their experience to yours, and when you feel comfortable leaving them, say goodbye, and come back to your awareness of this room.

Past-Life Regression Exercise II

Lie down, close your eyes and get comfortable, or if you are more comfortable in a lotus position, you may do that. You need to find a position that will be physically comfortable for you for about an hour's time. Past-life regression requires a lot of emotional and mental energy, so you need to provide yourself with a position which requires no physical energy to maintain. (As you move more deeply into the regression itself, you may begin to feel physically cold, so keep a light blanket handy.)

Hold a problem which you want to better understand in your mind. Think deeply about this problem. Allow yourself to experience all of the layers of emotional attachment you have to it. Try to analyze what troubling emotions you experience in connection to this problem. Is there sadness? Frustration? Anger? Resentment? Jealousy? Allow yourself to feel fully these emotions. (PAUSE.)

Take three deep breaths. As you exhale, imagine you are pushing these emotions out of your body. With each exhalation, feel more and more relaxed. (PAUSE.) Breathe once more, as long and deep as you can make it.

Now, imagine, if you will, a warm and brilliant beam of light coming down from above you and resting for a moment on the top of your head. This light is pure white, the color of life's essence. Feel its power filter down through your body. Allow your entire body to become bathed in this light. This light is here to enlighten and console you; it is here to provide insight and reassurance. The power of this light is always accessible and available to you whenever you feel the need for its comfort. Realize that the power and strength, the brilliance and wisdom of this light is by nature what you are. You are part of it, just as it is part of the universe in which you exist. It is as everlasting as you are. Acquaint yourself with this part of you. Feel how powerful, how loving, how wise, and how blissful it is to be this light, of which you are an inseparable part.

This light—which you may envision as your Higher self—will bring you understanding of who you are and why you exist as you do on this planet. It is here to give you reassurance and guidance into the problem you wish to address.

Imagine now that you are standing at the top of a long stairway. The stairs are richly carpeted, deep and soft under your tread, as you descend now, slowly, one step at a time, one, two, going deeper into yourself, three, four, you are more and more relaxed, five, six, more and more centered, seven, eight, more and more attuned to all that you are, nine, ten.

At the bottom of the stairs, a long hallway appears before you. It is also lushly carpeted. It feels soft and comfortable under your feet. The walls around you are beautifully decorated, rich and ornate. There is a soft, glowing light all around you, and quiet, gentle music. You feel so peaceful, so relaxed and serene. At the end of the hallway you find a large door. You notice right away how delicately sculpted and magnificent it is. You are fascinated by its design, the years and years of work and creative expression that seem to have made it what it is. You understand now that this is the door to your past, and that its beautiful design is your own. You see a handle on the door and you reach for it. You feel the solid weight of it in your hand. You turn it, expecting it to be difficult to open, but find, instead, that it opens quite easily. You go through the doorway and step out into a beautiful, soft light.

Look around you and stand comfortably within that lighted space. When you are ready to see them, you may look down at your feet and try to notice what sort of shoes you are wearing.

Do you feel yourself to be inside or outside? Examine with your senses the space around you. What is the temperature like? Is it light or dark around you? Are you alone or are there people nearby? Try and get a sense of what you are doing in this space. Do any images or words come to mind? Do you smell anything? Do you hear anything?

If you are experiencing absolutely nothing, I want you to once again picture yourself at the doorway. Surround yourself with white light and understand that you are completely safe in this light. Now walk through the door and begin again to try and sense the space around you.

Are you male or female? Old or young? If you are not sure, count to three, and then you'll be sure. Get a sense of your clothing. If you were able earlier to envision your shoes, just continue to follow your way up your body with your eyes. What kind of person are you? Timid or fearless? Excitable or placid by nature? What interests you? How do you make your living? If you're not sure, count to three, and then you'll be sure. What concerns you? Spend a few moments just getting a sense of what sort of personality you are.

If it's important to you, you may want to ask yourself or try to get a sense of what time you are in, the century and culture. If you're not sure, count to three, and you'll be sure.

Do you have a family? Anyone you are particularly close to? What is this person like and what sort of relationship do you have with them? If you are not sure, count to three, and then you'll be sure. Spend a few moments getting a sense of the sort of emotional ties you have to others in this life.

Now ask yourself why you have remembered this person and what their life has to do with yours. What their life has to do with the problem you held in your mind a few moments ago. Ask your Higher self this question. What does this prior life have to teach me about the problem I am having now? Count to five; the answer will come.

What other lessons were learned in this life? What reassurance can I have regarding my emotional confusion and trouble with this problem? Ask your Higher self if there is any other message?

Now, think for a moment about the troubles and sorrows experienced by the individual you have re-acquainted yourself with in this exercise. Forgive all of the pain that was caused them by others. Forgive all the mistakes they feel they made in their lifetime, and as the person you are now, send them love and compassion. Thank them for experiencing what they did and acknowledge the part of you that is them. Send love and forgiveness to that part of yourself.

Whenever you feel inclined to do so, you may turn your attention back to this life and the room you are in, and open your eyes.

To order more copies of *The Baroness, the Scribe and the Camel-Driver*, please enclose this order blank, your check or money order for $12.95 plus $2.00 shipping and handling to Ryse, Inc., P.O. Box 892, Monroe, CT., 06468.

Name_____

Address_____

City_____State*_____Zip_____

* (CT. residents, please add sales tax.)